GLOBETROTTER™

Travel G

C000059767

COSTA RICA

ROWLAND MEAD

NEW HOLLAND

NEW
HOLLAND

★★★ Highly recommended
★★ Recommended
★ See if you can

This edition first published in 2001
by New Holland Publishers (UK) Ltd
London • Cape Town • Sydney • Auckland
First edition published in 1999
10 9 8 7 6 5 4 3 2 1

Garfield House, 86 Edgware Road
London W2 2EA
United Kingdom

80 McKenzie Street
Cape Town 8001
South Africa

14 Aquatic Drive
Frenchs Forest, NSW 2086
Australia

218 Lake Road
Northcote, Auckland
New Zealand

Distributed in the USA by
The Globe Pequot Press
Connecticut

Copyright © 2001 in text: Rowland Mead
Copyright © 2001 in maps: Globetrotter Travel Maps
Copyright © 2001 in photographs:
Individual photographers as credited
Copyright © 1999, 2001 New Holland Publishers
(UK) Ltd

All rights reserved. No part of this publication
may be reproduced, stored in a retrieval system
or transmitted, in any form or by any means,
electronic, mechanical, photocopying, recording
or otherwise, without the prior written permission
of the publishers and copyright holders.

ISBN 185974 800 7

Commissioning Editor: Tim Jollands
Manager Globetrotter Maps: John Loubser

Managing Editor: Thea Grobbelaar
Editors: Tarryn Berry, Catherine Mallinick, Peter
Duncan, Thea Grobbelaar
Design and DTP: Nicole Engeler, Catherine Mallinick
Cartographer: Elaine Fick
Picture Researchers: Colleen Abrahams, Rowena Curtis

Reproduction by Hirt & Carter (Pty) Ltd, Cape Town
Printed and bound in Hong Kong by Sing Cheong
Printing Co. Ltd

Although every effort has been made to ensure
accuracy of facts, telephone and fax numbers in this
book, the publishers will not be held responsible for
changes that occur at the time of going to press.

Photographic Credits:
Axiom, 29, 32, 63, 112; Axiom/Ian Cumming, cover;
Frank Lane Picture Agency, 14; ICOMOS
Documentation Centre, Paris, 58; Life File/Flora
Torrance, 7, 24, 41, 78, 84, 90, 95, 96, 100, 101, 103, 111,
115, 116, 119; Rowland Mead, 77, 104, 105; Mary
Evans Picture Library, 17; Jeroen Snijders, title page,
4, 6, 8, 9, 11, 12, 13, 15, 19, 20, 21, 22, 23, 25, 26, 27, 28,
30, 31, 35, 36, 37, 38, 39, 40, 44, 47, 48, 49, 50, 51 (top
and bottom), 52, 53, 54, 55, 56, 57, 60, 64, 65, 66, 67, 68
(top and bottom), 69, 70, 71, 72, 74, 76, 79, 80, 81, 82,
83, 85, 86, 87, 88, 92, 93, 94, 97, 98, 99, 102, 106, 108,
113 (top and bottom), 114, 117; South American
Pictures, 16, 18, 118, 120.

Acknowledgements:
The author and publishers gratefully acknowledge
the valuable assistance in the compilation of this book
by Trips Worldwide, Bristol, UK (particularly Jo
Campbell) and Camino Travel, San José, Costa Rica
(especially Helena Chavarría). The author would also
like to thank Mauricio Hernandez of Camino Travel
for his help in updating this book.

Front Cover: *Tourists admire the forest from the Sky Walk
in the Monteverde area.*
Title Page: *Traditional ox cart, Sarchí.*

CONTENTS

1. Introducing Costa Rica 5
The Land 6
History in Brief 16
Government and Economy 22
The People 24

2. San José 33
Plaza de la Cultura and Around 34
East of the City Centre 37
North and Eastern Suburbs 40
Parque La Sabana and Escazú 41

3. The Central Valley and Surrounding Highlands 45
Alajuela and Around 46
Heredia 50
Braulio Carrillo National Park 52
Cartago and Around 53
Turrialba 57

4. The Caribbean Coast 61
Caribbean Lowlands 62
Puerto Limón 63
South from Puerto Limón 64
North from Puerto Limón 67

5. The Northern Zone 75
Puerto Viejo and Around 76
San Carlos 79
Fortuna and Lake Arenal 80
Caño Negro Wildlife Refuge 84
Monteverde Area 85

6. Guanacaste and the Southern Nicoya Peninsula 91
The Interamericana Route 92
Northern National Parks 96
Northern Nicoya Peninsula 98
Guanacaste Coast 100
Southern Nicoya Peninsula 104

7. The Southern Pacific Coast 109
Puntarenas 110
South from Puntarenas 111
Osa Peninsula 117
Golfito Area 119
Isla del Coco National Park 120

Travel Tips 122
Index 127

1
Introducing Costa Rica

Located in the Central American isthmus between Nicaragua and Panama, tiny Costa Rica, only a quarter the size of Scotland, packs an amazing diversity into its 51,120km² (19, 739 sq miles). Its high mountain ranges, reaching 3820m (12,533ft) at **Mt Chirripó**, give rise to a variety of climate and vegetation zones. The **Caribbean coast** is hot, steamy and covered with **rain forest**, while in the west the **Pacific coast** is drier, with cattle ranching predominating. Inland, the **Central Valley** is surrounded by **volcanoes**, many benignly active. Their ash has weathered into fertile soil ideal for the production of **coffee**, for many years Costa Rica's main export.

Costa Rica has become one of the world's prime **eco-tourism** destinations – helped by the fact that 27 per cent of the countryside is protected to some degree. **Activity holidays** also have a big following, with scuba diving, hiking, surfing and big game fishing all highly popular.

Above all, however, tourists perceive Costa Rica to be **safe**. It has been a **democracy** for over 100 years and abolished its armed forces after the Civil War in 1948, remaining free of the coups and dictatorships which beleaguer neighbouring countries. In recognition of this, over 35,000 North American citizens have settled here.

The estimated population of Costa Rica is 3.5 million, around one tenth of whom live in **San José**, the capital. Catholicism is the main religion and this is still a strongly family-orientated society. The Costa Ricans refer to themselves as *ticos* and their warmth always leaves a lasting impression on visitors to this fascinating country.

TOP ATTRACTIONS

*** Tortuguero Channels: Caribbean coastal canals through the rain forest.
*** Rain Forest Aerial Tram: chair lift through the canopy near Braulio Carrillo National Park.
*** Poás Volcano National Park: views directly into the volcano's crater from its rim.
*** Monteverde Cloud Forest: trails through the ultimate cloud forest.
** National Theatre: built in San José by wealthy 19th-century coffee barons.
** Pacific Coast Beaches: for sunsets and water sports.

Opposite: *Rain forest fringes a beach on Costa Rica's Pacific coast.*

FACTS AND FIGURES

• **Size:** Costa Rica is the second smallest of the Central American republics, covering 19,739 sq miles (51,000km²).
• **Provinces:** there are seven provinces, Limón, Cartago, Heredia, Alajuela, Guanacaste, Puntarenas and San José.
• **Population:** a 1999 estimate was 3,622,171.
• **Annual Population Growth:** 1.78 per cent (1999).
• **GNP per capita:** US$3.302
• **Road Network:** extensive, but only 15% is paved.
• **Highest Mountain:** Mt. Chirripó 3820m (12,533 ft). Although it lies within the tropics, frost is common on the summit at night.
• **Longest river:** Rio San Juan, which forms part of the border with Nicaragua.

Below: *The Tortuguero area on the Caribbean coast abounds with canals, rivers and creeks.*

THE LAND

Costa Rica is situated within the **tropics**, between latitudes 8°N and 11°N. Its borders are contained by the Pacific Ocean in the west and the Caribbean Sea in the east. To the north is **Nicaragua** and to the south, **Panama**.

Costa Rica owes its physical origin to the movement of **plates** in the earth's crust. In the recent geological past, part of the Pacific Plate, known as the Cocos Plate, moved against the Caribbean Plate forming a 'collision zone', resulting in the upfolding of rocks into mountains and the outpouring of volcanic material. This eventually formed an **isthmus** or land bridge linking the continents of North and South America, a passage which was used by wildlife and eventually humans. Costa Rica remains on the plate boundary today and volcanoes and frequent earthquakes are typical of this unstable zone.

Mountains and Rivers

Some 60 **volcanoes** can be identified and of these eight have been recently active. They occur in four ranges, which run in a northwest/southeast direction from the Nicaraguan to the Panama border. In the northwest is the **Cordillera de Guanacaste**, with a long string of volcanoes, including Volcán Orosí (1487m; 4785ft), Volcán Santa María (1916m; 6286ft) and Volcán Rincón de

la Vieja (1895m; 6217ft). Further southeast is the **Cordillera de Tilarán**, with the active Volcán Arenal (1633m; 5358ft) and this mountain chain then merges into the **Cordillera Central**, with a number of volcanoes which can be seen from the capital, San José. These include the accessible Volcán Poás (2704m; 8871ft), Volcán Irazú (3432m; 11,260ft)

and Volcán Barva (2906m; 9534ft). The fourth chain is the **Cordillera de Talamanca**. This huge granite batholith's uplift led to the formation of Costa Rica's highest mountain, Cerro Chirripó (3820m; 12,533ft). Within the mountain chains lies the **Central Valley**, a plateau at a height of between 1000m (3280ft) and 1500m (4920ft). The landscape here is formed of volcanic soil, which, along with the amenable climate of the Central Valley, has led to the location here of four of the five main cities of Costa Rica.

On either side of the Central Valley and the highlands are **coastal lowlands**. To the east lie the **Caribbean Lowlands**, a generally flat area crossed by rivers, such as the Reventazón and the Chirripó. Much of the rain forest vegetation here has been cleared for agriculture.

The **Pacific Lowlands**, on the other hand, are more undulating. The pronounced dry season gives savannah and dry tropical forest land, on which cattle ranching thrives. Numerous rivers flow west off the cordilleras, such as the Río Tempisque in the north, flowing into the **Gulf of Nicoya**. Further south, the main river is the Térraba, which has formed a delta in the Bay of Coronado.

Above: *Volcán Orosí is one of eight active volcanoes in Costa Rica, most of which can be approached safely.*

VOLCANOES

Volcanoes are mountains formed by hot molten material which is forced through weak points in the earth's crust. The material may be liquid, as in the case of **lava**, or solid, as with volcanic **bombs** or **ash**. Both steam and gases are also commonly found around volcanoes. Those volcanoes which are erupting at the present time are known as **active**, while those which are totally dead are called **extinct**. Volcanoes which are temporarily quiet are said to be **dormant**.

DISAPPEARING REEFS

Coral reefs are underwater banks of limestone, formed by filter-feeding animals known as polyps. Polyps need clear, unpolluted salt water to survive. In Costa Rica, they are found only along the Caribbean coast, especially in the **Cahuita National Park** and around Isla del Coco. The coral reefs are, however, fast disappearing, for three main reasons. Increased logging has resulted in soil erosion. The resulting mud eventually reaches the sea and the particles then block up the feeding systems of the polyps. Secondly, after deforestation, trees are replaced by bananas or oil palms. The chemicals used on these plantations are washed into the sea, killing the coral. The third factor was the 1991 earthquake, which raised the sea bed by over a metre, killing stretches of the reef.

Seas and Shores

The Pacific and Caribbean coastlines present marked contrasts. The **Caribbean Coast** is short, stretching for little over 200km (125 miles) and is characterized by sandy beaches, backed by mangroves and rain forest. Offshore, particularly in the south, are occasional coral reefs, but many of these have been destroyed as recent earth movements have raised their levels. An intra-coastal waterway runs parallel to the shore in the north, providing local people with their main form of communication. The **Pacific Coast**, in contrast, stretches for over 1000km (620 miles) and is generally rugged, with headlands interspersed with mangroves and sandy beaches. There are two important peninsulas running parallel to the coast. In the north, the **Península de Nicoya** is backed by the Gulf of Nicoya, while in the south the **Osa Peninsula** protects the Golfo Dulce. The combination of favourable climate and attractive scenery has led to the development of a thriving tourist industry on the Pacific coast. There are also islands off the Pacific coast, including the **Isla del Coco**, some 532km (330 miles) from the mainland. Covering 24km² (9 sq miles), it is believed to be the largest uninhabited island in the world.

Climate

As a subtropical country, Costa Rica experiences two seasons. The **dry season** lasts from December to April and is known as *verano* (summer), while the remainder of the year comprises the **wet season** called *invierno* (winter). Some areas experience a short dry spell some time between July and September, known as the *veranillo* (little summer). Having said that, there are considerable differences depending on position and altitude. The Caribbean lowlands, for example, receive rain throughout the year, often recording over 500cm (200in), a pattern repeated in the southern Pacific area, although rainfall totals there are lower. The driest and hottest part of the country is Guanacaste Province in the northwest, where temperatures often reach 40°C (104°F), while the coldest area is the peak of Chirripó, which frequently experiences temperatures below freezing point. The most agreeable climate to be found in Costa Rica is in the Central Valley, where temperatures average a healthy 20°C (68°F) throughout the year.

The higher peaks of the cordilleras are often cloud-covered and tourists visiting the more popular volcanoes should do so early in the morning before the mists descend. The dry season is the peak period for tourism, both for foreigners and Costa Ricans. Accommodation charges are highest at this time and advanced booking for hotels is recommended, particularly at weekends. However, the authorities in Costa Rica are trying hard to extend the tourist year by referring to the wet season as the **Green Season**. Certainly, it does not rain all the time and mornings can often be dry. The resorts will not be crowded, but in some parts of the country access may be limited because of flooded roads, rivers and landslides. A 4WD vehicle is essential when travelling at this time.

Above: *Many of the country's volcanoes and higher ranges are swathed in mist for a large part of the time, leading to the formation of 'cloud forest'.*
Opposite: *The Pacific coast features some superb beaches, none better than those in the Manuel Antonio National Park.*

RAIN FOREST DESTRUCTION

Rain forests occur in areas up to ten degrees either side of the Equator and form a habitat for between 40% and 50% of all living land creatures. Despite this they are being destroyed. Some experts take the view that by 2010, little rain forest will be left outside the protected areas. Others point out that the remaining forests must be **sustainable**, either through tourism, investment by the developed world, or pharmaceutical production.

Flora

The diversity of flora in Costa Rica is astounding. The country is part of a narrow land bridge between North and South America and therefore has species from both continents. The variety in climate and altitude adds to this a large number of different **life zones**, producing habitats such as forest, mangroves and wetlands. Finally, up to 27 per cent of the country's land is protected.

Some 10,000 species of plants have been recorded in Costa Rica, including 1200 types of **orchid**, one of which is the national emblem of the country. Over 1400 species of tree have been noted, many of which are in the tropical rain forests. Here, the diversity of species is astounding and it is often possible to identify over 200 types of tree within one acre. Trees also support other plant life such

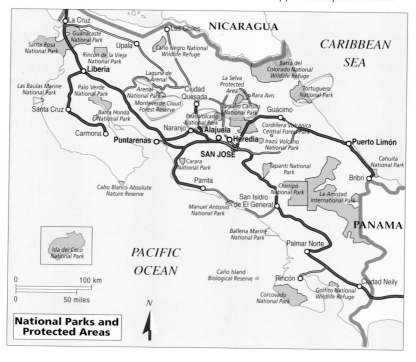

National Parks and Protected Areas

as **epiphytes**, **bromeliads** and **lianas**. Many trees are valuable hardwoods such as teak and rosewood, and illegal logging still goes on, despite official protection. The secondary forest which grows after clearance rarely has the variety and number of species found in the primary forest.

Above: *Over 1400 species of trees can be found in the rain forest, often festooned with orchids and epiphytes.*

Mammals

There are some 240 species of mammals in Costa Rica, half of which are bats. All visitors to the rain forests hope to spot the **wildcats**, such as jaguars, margays, ocelots and pumas, but these are elusive and rarely seen. The same applies to the pig-like **tapir**, a distant relative of the rhinoceros with a prehensile snout, which can weigh up to 300kg (660 lb). **Monkeys** are more noticeable and the visitor is most likely to see the howler, which will noisily defend its territory. Rather rarer are the delicate white-faced, spider and squirrel monkeys. Expertly camouflaged in the rain forests are the slow-moving **sloths,** of which there are two types in Costa Rica. The three-toed sloth is active by day, while the two-toed sloth is nocturnal. Sloths' main predators are eagles, but they are most at risk when they descend, once a week, to the forest floor to defecate.

Other interesting mammals include **anteaters**, of which there are three local varieties. They are unique in that they have no teeth, but use a long, sticky tongue to take in their main diet of ants and termites. The largest is the giant anteater, which can reach 2m (6ft) in length and has a tongue which protrudes up to 60cm (20in). More common is the lesser anteater, which is adept at climbing the forest trees, using its strong tail. The silky anteater is nocturnal and rarely seen, but is reputed to devour up to 6000 ants in one night. Finally, there are the related **armadillos**, of which there are two species in Costa Rica, having migrated originally from the South American continent. Armadillos are

---

EPIPHYTES

Tropical rain forests are generally described as having four layers, a canopy; a subcanopy; an understorey; and a shrub layer. A feature of the first three strata is the epiphyte, and plants of this species are common in Costa Rican rain forests. Epiphytes may be described as 'plants which grow on other plants', having no roots in the ground. The most common types are the ferns, mosses and lichens, but there are more exotic species, such as orchids. Some types of epiphyte are parasitic – they live 'off' the tree as well as 'on' it, taking nutrients from the host. These include the bromeliads, which resemble the leafy part of an upturned pineapple. Their leaves trap and store moisture, a supply often used by creatures of the forest for drinking.

COSTA RICAN MONKEYS

There are four monkey species in Costa Rica, all in the family Cebidae. The **howler monkey's** chilling roar is said to be the loudest in the animal world. The most inquisitive are **white faced capuchin** monkeys who forage in groups at all levels of the forest. **Spider monkeys** have long arms and legs and a prehensile tail. The tiny **squirrel monkeys** are confined to the Manuel Antonio and Corcovado National Parks.

Below: *The green lizard is just one of a huge number of amphibians and reptiles to be found countrywide.*
Opposite: *Costa Rica has around 10 per cent of the world's butterflies and supplies pupae to butterfly farms in many countries.*

unusual in that their bodies have bands of pliable protective plates, while, equally curiously, their offspring emerge as identical quadruplets hatching from a single egg.

Amphibians and Reptiles

Costa Rica boasts many brightly coloured **frogs** and toads, particularly in the rain forests. They are often small, such as the tree frogs, many of which are no bigger than a thumbnail, but their gaudy colours betray their poisonous nature. The rain forest waterways are often the haunt of **caimans** and **crocodiles**, though these rarely reach a size which make them dangerous to man. A remarkable amphibian is the basilisk or **'Jesus Christ' lizard**, which patters over the water when disturbed. The most widespread lizard is the iguana, of which there are a number of species. They are found in a wide variety of habitats, some even being found in hotel grounds, where they can become very tame.

Costa Rica has five species of **sea turtle** – the Olive Ridley, loggerhead, hawksbill, green and huge leatherback. They nest mainly at night, when they come ashore in large numbers, an event known as an *arribada*. In addition, there are fresh water turtles in the rivers and mangrove swamps. Finally Costa Rica boasts no less than 162 species of snakes, of which 22 are venomous. Most, however, are shy or nocturnal, and are rarely seen.

Insects

Few tourists will fail to be impressed by Costa Rica's butterflies. Some 10 per cent of the world's total may be seen here, including the stunning **blue morpho**, which can measure 20cm (8in) across. It makes a marvellous sight as it glides through rain forest clearings, yet when it lands, it folds its wings so that the brown speckled underwing makes it almost invisible amongst the foliage. Less welcome are mosquitoes, some of which carry Dengue fever and malaria. On the forest floor, the **leaf cutter ants** are always busy, carrying material to their nests. The larger bullet ants, however, should be avoided as their bite can be painful.

Birds

Costa Rica has become something of a Mecca for bird watchers in recent years and many tourists have bird watching high on their list of holiday activities. Including migratory birds, an incredible 850 species have been recorded, comprising many fine specimens and rarities. The bird which most foreign enthusiasts come to see is the **resplendent quetzal**. Highly regarded by the Maya and the Aztecs, its long tail feathers were used both in head-dresses and as currency. Today, this brightly coloured bird, possessing a 1.5m (4ft) long tail, is becoming increasingly rare, but can fortunately still be found in the Monteverde Cloud Forest and on the Osa Peninsula, both its natural habitats. Other exotic (and noisy) birds to be seen include the **scarlet macaw**, **toucans** and a whole range of **parrots** and parakeets.

JUNGLE CATS

It is the ambition of every wildlife enthusiast who visits Costa Rica to see a **jaguar**. This large spotted cat was revered by the ancient Indians of Central America and often figures on their pottery. Today, because of the large forest territory it requires, it has become endangered. The other large cat is the plain brown **puma** or mountain lion. Smaller spotted cats include the **ocelot**, the **margay** and the rare **oncilla**. Finally, a dark brown cat with a long tail and short legs will be a **jaguarundi**. All the cats are endangered and shy – the visitor will need both luck and patience to spot one.

RESPLENDENT QUETZAL

Described as one of the most beautiful birds on earth, the resplendent quetzal of Costa Rica has a bright red breast, an emerald green back and wings and a bold, spiky, helmet-like crest. The male's most distinguishing feature is a pair of iridescent long green tail feathers. However, many bird watchers leave the country without seeing the beautiful bird. The quetzal lives in the canopy of the cloud forest areas and is therefore difficult to spot. Due to deforestation, it is now also an endangered species. The best places to view the quetzal are the Tapanti Wildlife Refuge and the Chirripó National Park.

Hummingbirds are one of the most common bird varieties in Costa Rica and can often be seen enjoying nectar from flowers while hovering. There are over 50 species of hummingbird, some of which migrate to America for the northern summer. Numerous and pretty **songbirds**, such as tanagers and flycatchers, follow the same route.

Water and wetland birds are common and easily observed by bird watchers. Few beaches are without their brown **pelicans** diving into the surf, often close to surfers and swimmers, while royal terns and magnificent frigatebirds patrol overhead. In the stillness of the swamps and mangroves, members of the **heron** family are frequent and approachable. They include the night heron, egrets, great blue heron, tiger heron and bitterns. Other exotic waterbirds to be found are ibises, spoonbills and storks. **Anhingas** or 'snakebirds' are often seen drying their wings in the mangroves or on mooring posts, while there are four varieties of kingfisher to be commonly seen along the waterways.

Amongst the **raptors**, the most likely to be noticed are the black hawk, the broad winged hawk and the aptly named laughing falcon. Ospreys are still common along the rain forest waterways, but the bushy crowned harpy eagle is rapidly facing extinction and sadly only a few pairs may still be seen in the Osa Peninsula. Finally, one of the most widespread species of bird in Costa Rica is the **vulture**, seen either as a reeling speck in the sky or waiting hopefully on a roadside tree for a squashed animal. Of the three vulture varieties, the black vulture is the most common.

Fish

Costa Rica is one of the most popular **sportfishing** venues in the world, with tarpon, marlin, snook and wahoo in abundance. The most popular locations are the waters of Barra del Colorado on the Caribbean coast, and Quepos and Golfito on the Pacific coast. Freshwater fish include trout and rainbow bass.

Sharks are not uncommon, particularly near beaches where turtles nest. **Dolphins** and **whales** are occasionally seen, particularly near the Ballena Marine National Park, where sperm and humpback whales may pass through in April and May. There also several coral reef habitats, abounding with small, colourful fish, most notably around the distant Isla del Coco in the Pacific.

Eco-tourism

Over half the visitors to Costa Rica come to see the abundant wildlife, and many local tourist agencies run **eco-lodges**, frequently near or around National Parks or in rain forest locations. It is also often advisable to hire local guides, who will be experts on the wildlife of their area.

HUMMINGBIRDS

Of the 330 species of hummingbird found in the New World, some 51 can be identified in Costa Rica and visitors will be extremely unlucky not to see several species during their stay. Hummingbirds are generally small, 6–20cm (2–8in), with iridescent colours and a flight which involves extremely rapid wing beats. Uniquely, the entire wing can rotate at the shoulder joint, enabling the bird to hover, fly backwards or sideways, in order to extract nectar from tubular flowers. The bill of the hummingbird is varied in size and shape to cope with their preferred flower. Needless to say, these birds are vitally important pollinators, particularly in colder areas where insect and bat activity tends to be limited.

Left: *Costa Rican children are taught to appreciate the wildlife of their country and many keep pet birds and other animals.*
Opposite: *The resplendent quetzal is probably the most exotic of the 850 species of bird which can be spotted in Costa Rica.*

LITHIC SPHERES

One of the great unsolved mysteries of Costa Rica is the existence, in the south of the country, of numbers of lithic spheres or stone balls (*esferas de piedra*). Almost exactly circular in shape, they are found in the Diquis region and were probably made by the *indigenas* of the same name. They vary in size from a tennis ball to as much as 2m (6ft) across and are composed of hard rock such as granite. The spheres are often found at religious sites, such as burial grounds, and appear to have been placed in set positions. In other places there seems no reason for their location. How were the spheres made, bearing in mind the technology of the time? How were they moved across the countryside? What was the purpose behind their careful placing? They can be seen in the National Museum and parks in San José, as well as in the south. Some of the more affluent *ticos* even have them as garden features .

Below: *Mysterious lithic or stone spheres are found in many parts of the country.*

HISTORY IN BRIEF
Pre-Columbian Times

The land which is now Costa Rica was probably first peopled around 10,000BC, but it is only from about 1000BC that any real evidence has emerged of the way of life of these people. When the Spaniards arrived in the 16th century, they found between 20 and 30 tribes, who they named after the chief or *cacique* with whom they negotiated. So, for instance, there were the **Capatas** in the north, the **Guayamis** and the **Térrebas** in the south and the **Huetars** in the Central Valley. More advanced were the **Chorotegas** in what is now Guanacaste province. The most remarkable remnants of this time, however, are the stone spheres which come from the Diquis region in the southwest of the country. Made of granite and measuring up to 2m (6ft) in radius, their purpose remains uncertain and no one has been able to explain how they managed to reach the Isla del Caño, some 20km (12 miles) offshore.

Living in stockaded villages, these indigenous people practised subsistence farming. Religion was evidently important, the shaman being the most revered member of the group after the *cacique*. Gender divisions were traditional, with women largely confined to a domestic role. The tribes were almost constantly at war with each other and, as no group was able to gain complete ascendancy, they remained fragmented. The purpose of the warfare was not to increase territory but rather to capture slaves, wives or victims for religious sacrifice.

The most important archaeological site from these pre-Columbian times is the Monumento Nacional Guayabo, located 85km (53 miles) to the east of San José. Believed to have been occupied between AD1000 and AD1400, it is estimated to have housed as many as 20,000 inhabitants and is thought to have been an important religious centre. There are remains of ancient roadways, aqueducts and buildings, while jade and gold jewellery and other artefacts have been found.

The Spanish Conquest

The Spanish arrival began on 18 September 1502 when Christopher Columbus, on his fourth and last voyage to the New World, landed near the present day Puerto Limón. His party stayed for 17 days and were very warmly received by the indigenous people, who, Columbus noted in his journals, were

wearing gold jewellery and decorations. He then sailed off to continue his explorations.

Four years later, King Ferdinand of Spain appointed Diego de Nicuesa to colonize and govern the area. This time around the local people were overtly hostile to the Spaniards, while the colonists found the rain forest equally forbidding and dangerous, so the expedition was eventually abandoned.

Above: *Christopher Columbus gave Costa Rica its name, mistakenly believing that the land was rich in gold and other precious minerals.*

HISTORICAL CALENDAR

c10,000BC The first human inhabitants moved into what is now the country of Costa Rica.
c1000BC Organized societies formed, with groups led by *caciques*, who traded and fought with each other and maintained links with other civilizations in South and Central America.
1502 Columbus landed on the Costa Rican coast near what is today Puerto Limón.
1519–1561 Spanish explore both the Pacific and Caribbean coasts.
1561 A Spanish expedition

reaches the Central Valley and founds the settlement which eventually becomes Cartago.
1572 Coronado explores the Central Valley and the colonial era begins.
1737 San José is founded.
late 1700s Coffee is first grown as a cash crop.
1821 Costa Rica and the other Central American republics gain their independence from Spain.
1838 Costa Rica becomes an independent republic with San José as its capital.
1856 Costa Ricans overcome William Walker's invasion.

1889 First democratic elections held.
1899 United Fruit company founded by Minor Keith, who also built the Jungle Railway to Puerto Limón.
1949 After the failed revolution, the army is disbanded.
1987 President Arias awarded the Nobel Peace Prize for his efforts to bring peace to Central America.
1994 José Figueres becomes Costa Rica's youngest President, at the age of 39.
1998 Miguel Angel Rodríguez elected as President

Above: *A monument celebrates the defeat of William Walker in 1855.*

CHRISTOPHER COLUMBUS

Known as Cristóbal Colón in Spain, Columbus is credited as being the first European to discover Costa Rica and give the country its name. He lived in the conviction that the East Indies could be reached by sailing westwards and he eventually persuaded monarchs Ferdinand and Isabel to finance an exploratory voyage. He set out with three small vessels and eventually made landfall in what is now the Bahamas. His second voyage was a grander affair with 17 vessels and 1500 men, who set up a number of colonies. The third ended in the ignominy of being returned to Spain in irons. During his last voyage, in 1502, he made landfall in what is now Costa Rica. Continuing his explorations, he was shipwrecked and taken back to Spain, where he died three years later.

There were further attempts at colonization and for the next 30 years the *indigenas* mounted a prolonged and effective campaign of resistance. By the 1560s, however, the conquest was complete, helped by the common diseases brought by the Europeans, which effectively decimated the native people. During the 17th century, the numbers of *indigenas* dropped alarmingly from around 80,000 to scarcely 10,000, which had serious implications for the colonists, as they had little slave labour to work the mines and till the soil.

By now, led by the Governor Juan Vásquez de Coronado, a successful colony had been formed in the Central Valley, where there was a healthy climate and fertile soil. Cartago was founded in 1563 as the capital of the area, though this was often described as the 'forgotten colony', as it developed in a very different way from other conquered territories. Far from the sea and largely divorced from mainstream Spanish influence, the settlers had no local workforce and were unable to intermarry with the indigenous people to set up the *mestizo* culture found in other parts of Latin America. Poverty was widespread, valuable minerals were non-existent and the remote position of the colony did not lend itself to trading, so most of the settlers were obliged to turn to subsistence farming. These unusual and challenging conditions, it is often argued, led to the country's modern egalitarian society.

Urban growth in Costa Rica was slow. Cartago was largely destroyed by a volcanic eruption but was rebuilt by the survivors. Heredia was founded in 1717, San José followed in 1737 and then Alajuela in 1782. After a minor civil war in the early part of the 19th century, the capital was moved to San José.

Independence

When, in 1823, Spain granted independence to the colonies of Central America, Costa Rica joined the Central American Federation. However, it withdrew its membership in 1838 to become an independent state. Its first President was Juan Mora Fernández and during his time in office, coffee, which had been introduced in 1808, began to be exported and was soon the country's main trading item and a profitable source of income. Inevitably a wealthy **coffee bourgeoisie** developed, who were powerful enough to elect their own president, Juan Rafael Mora.

Despite the economic growth during his presidency, Mora is best known for a bizarre incident, when an American filibuster, William Walker, arrived in Nicaragua in 1855 with the intention of overcoming the whole of Central America and turning it into a slave colony. Mora mobilized an 'army' of 9000 civilians and defeated Walker just over the border in Nicaragua. Walker escaped, but later returned to the area several times, before being executed in Honduras in 1860. Mora, meanwhile, became less popular, and after a coup he was eventually himself executed, ironically in the same year as Walker.

WILLIAM WALKER

Born in Tennessee, William Walker was one of the most outlandish figures of 19th-century Central America. He conceived a plan, apparently with US President Buchanan's backing, of invading Central America and setting up a slave colony. The slaves would build a canal through Nicaragua linking the Pacific to the Caribbean. He invaded Costa Rica with mercenaries but President Mora's ragtag army of *campesinos* drove him out of the country. He later spent three years in a Nicaraguan jail. Undeterred, he invaded Honduras in 1860, claiming the presidency. He was caught and swiftly executed.

Below: *The now obsolete five colones note is depicted on a beach towel.*

PEACE BROKER OF CENTRAL AMERICA

Costa Rica managed to avoid the political conflict of its Central American neighbours during the 1980s and early 1990s. Much of this was due to **President Oscar Arias Sánchez**, who saw that if peace was to be maintained in his country, then a regional solution was necessary. He therefore played a peace broker role to attempt to solve conflicts in Nicaragua, Honduras, Guatemala and El Salvador, proposing cease fires, the cessation of military aid to rebels, the release of political prisoners and amnesties for guerrillas. He also encouraged the holding of democratic elections. Arias' actions did not always meet with the approval of the US, but he used his diplomatic credibility to secure aid to meet Costa Rica's international debts and gained funds to underpin the country's educational and health systems. Arias was awarded the Nobel Peace Prize in 1987, bringing international recognition to Costa Rica. He was less popular in home affairs, being accused of repeatedly diverting resources to foreign affairs.

Democracy

The first democratic elections in Costa Rica were held in 1889 and apart from a few minor 'blips', the country has remained a democracy ever since. Economic stability underpinned this political situation, with coffee exports to Europe becoming increasingly important. In 1890, a railway was completed from San José to the Caribbean coast, which made the export of coffee beans far easier. The railway, known as the **Jungle Train**, took 20 years to build and some 4000 workers lost their lives during its construction. Towards the end of the project, with funds running short, the American engineer, Minor Keith, planted bananas along the lower part of the route to raise money to complete the line. Unexpectedly, the plantations quickly flourished and bananas became an important export crop for Costa Rica. Keith himself formed the **United Fruit Company**, which was to revolutionize labour relations and have important social, economic and political implications throughout the Central American region.

Right: *Election days in Costa Rica are always a public holiday and usually turn into a lively 'political fiesta'; even prisoners are allowed to vote.*

The Twentieth Century

The early years of the 20th century were often unstable, but democracy survived. The two World Wars hit coffee exports, though hostilities did not affect the region directly. The year 1948 proved an important one in Costa Rica's history, when a defeated candidate for the presidency refused to accept the result. This led to **Civil War** and a junta led

by José Pepe Figueres took over the country. A new constitution was drafted and Figueres handed over to the rightfully elected president. The constitution gave votes to women and blacks and abolished Costa Rica's army.

The 1970s and 1980s were stormy times in Central America, with political conflict in many countries, such as neighbouring Nicaragua, El Salvador, Honduras and Guatemala. In 1986, the Costa Rican president, **Oscar Arias Sánchez**, formulated a Peace Plan to bring stability to the region. Although his efforts met with mixed success, he was awarded the **Nobel Peace Prize**. Nicaraguan *contras* resident in the country were expelled and Costa Rica's official policy of neutrality was reinforced. In 1994 **José María Figueres**, the son of Don Pepe, was elected to president. His main problems concerned Costa Rica's economy, the stability of which has always been linked with the world prices of coffee and bananas. Inflation for the year 2000 is expected to be around 10 per cent, while population growth has risen by over three per cent a year, before stabilizing now at 1.78 per cent. Fortunately, **tourism** continues to fuel the economy. In February 1998, **Miguel Angel Rodríguez** was elected President. An economist, he aims to improve the country's infrastructure, create opportunities for the less fortunate in society and privatize state-run industries. A president is elected for a four-year term, so Rodríguez will wnd his term in 2002.

Above: *Panoramic view of San José, which was founded in 1737 and has been the capital of Costa Rica for over 150 years.*

VISITING NATIONAL PARKS

Most national parks in Costa Rica can be entered without a permit, but an entrance fee is payable on arrival. The fee was quite modest until 1994, when it was dramatically raised, causing something of a furore. Following criticism, the fee was then lowered to a more reasonable rate, but today, Costa Ricans still pay only ⅙ the cost of foreigners. The fee currently stands at $6, and there are no reduced rates. For information, contact the **Sistema Nacional de Areas de Conservación (SINAC)**, tel: 283-8004.

**A FIESTA OF THE
POLITICAL KIND**

General and Presidential
Elections in democratic Costa
Rica take place every four
years on the first Sunday in
February. The *ticos*, who love
a celebration, have contrived
over the years to turn voting
day into a kind of political
fiesta. Supporters of the two
main parties, the PLN and the
PUSC, fly the flags on their
houses and cars. Convoys of
vehicles tour the countryside
tooting their horns and *ticos*
take the opportunity to have a
meal out with their family.
Even prisoners are allowed to
vote, providing they have
registered, and often those
who have been released
return to jail to cast their vote.

Below: *Coffee beans are a major source of revenue for Costa Rica; tours around the coffee* fincas *are popular excursions for visitors.*

GOVERNMENT AND ECONOMY

The **Government** consists of a **Legislative Assembly**
with 57 deputies, elected by proportional representation
for four years and each serving approximately 30,000
people. Executive authority is in the hands of the president, assisted by two vice presidents; there is also a
cabinet of 18 ministers. Neither president nor deputies
can serve for more than one four-year term successively
(although there are plans to extend this period). There
are two main parties, the *Partido de Liberación Nacional*
(PLN) and the Social Christian Union Party (PUSC),
who in recent years have tended to alternate in power. In
the 1994 elections, for example, the PLN won a narrow
victory, with the PUSC returning in 1998. Voting is
mandatory for all Costa Rican citizens over the age of 18.

The basis of the **economy** is the export of agricultural
produce, particularly coffee and bananas. Meat, sugar
and cocoa are other traditional exports. There has been
more diversification in agricultural economy in recent
years, with house plants, seafood and fruit such as
pineapples featuring in the export charts. The industrial
sector has also grown rapidly during the last two
decades and exports now include pharmaceutical
products, tyres and textiles. Trade is overwhelmingly
with the USA, which takes 55 per cent of exports and
provides 43 per cent of Costa Rica's imports. Trade is
increasing with Europe and Asia. Recent
industrial projects include a petro-chemical
plant at Moín and a tuna processing plant at
Golfito. Costa Rica's major port is now Caldera
on the Pacific coast, which has been enlarged to
take cruise liners and container vessels.

Costa Rica has more mineral wealth than was
first realized, with considerable deposits of
bauxite, iron ore and sulphur, but little development has taken place. Gold is still mined on a
small scale in the southwest of the country.
A large part of Costa Rica's electricity require-
ments is catered for by the hydroelectric plant at
Lake Arenal. There are no oil deposits onshore but

some oil companies have bought up off-shore concessions in the Pacific. Costa Rica's only existing oil refinery is on the Caribbean coast at Puerto Limón.

Since the early 1990s, **tourism** has been the country's main foreign currency earner. Visitor numbers doubled between 1989 and 1993 and in 1999

levelled out at around 1, 027,462 annually, with a revenue of around US$1.001 million. The growth of tourism has led to much debate in Costa Rica about how the industry should develop. Most of the new hotels have been small, eco-lodge buildings, but the government has allowed foreign developers to build some mega-resorts on the Pacific coast, reversing what has been former policy.

Above: *Rain forest lodges have become an essential part of the eco-tourist's quest to be close to nature.*

Social Services

Healthcare in Costa Rica is of a high standard. Social Security hospitals will provide free emergency treatment for both locals and foreigners, while most prescription drugs are available at pharmacies. Private medical care is also widely available and there are some excellent private medical clinics in San José. Costs are lower than abroad and there is a trend for North Americans to come to Costa Rica on 'health holidays' for their dental treatment and cosmetic surgery.

Standards in **education** are also high and 6. 5 per cent of the national budget goes in this direction. Costa Rica has the highest literacy rate at 95 per cent (in people older than 12) in Central America. Education is compulsory up to the age of 14 years and there are some 60,231 students in higher education, with many in public universities, and some in private universities.

LIFE EXPECTANCY

The annual report of the World Health Organization (1997) showed that the **life expectancy** for Costa Ricans is currently 76.1 years. This is one of the highest rates in the world, comparing favourably with neighbouring countries. The rate is the second highest in the Americas, after Canada. The reasons for the high life expectancy are low infant mortality, low child mortality, good drinking water, adequate sewage disposal and close control of contagious illnesses. The agreeable climate of the Central Valley, where most *ticos* live, plus the healthy diet, are other important factors.

Above: *In more remote areas the horse is still a common form of transport.*
Opposite: *The family remains a strong social unit in Costa Rica.*

THE PEOPLE

The lastest census in 1999 estimated the population of Costa Rica at 3,622,171 million, with population growth being around 1.28 cent per annum. Life expectancy is at 76.1 per cent, infant mortality is low and child mortality lower still.

The population is ethnically homogenic, with 96 per cent of the people of Spanish descent. Some two per cent are black, but in Limón province this figure rises to 33 per cent, where their ancestry can be traced back to the West Indians brought over for the building of the Jungle Railway in the latter part of the last century. Many stayed to work on the banana plantations and their successors still speak an English patois. It was not until 1949, however, that they received equal rights with other Costa Ricans. Figures show that students of West Indian origin consistently outperform other Costa Ricans.

The indigenous population is now very small, no more than one per cent of the total, but there may be approximately 40,000 *mestizos* who have interbred and been assimilated into mainstream Costa Rican society. Some purebred *indigenas* live on reservations, mainly in the southern region of the country.

The Costa Ricans have been joined, in recent years, by up to 35,000 foreigners, mainly North Americans, who have decided to settle in the country. The locals like to call themselves *ticos* (f. *ticas*), which is at least less cumbersome than *costarricense*! The term comes from their habit of adding a diminutive to the end of a word, denoting familiarity or affection and therefore, it is claimed, reinforcing the idea of classlessness.

EDUCATION

At present, around 6.5% of the national budget finds its way into education. In fact, education in Costa Rica has been compulsory since 1869 and students must attend until the ninth grade, which is at the age of 14. As a result the country has the highest literacy rate in Latin America (95%). Large numbers of urban children go to pre-school classes. There are 3442 primary schools and about 200 secondary schools. The higher education sector is strong, with 6 universities. The problem concerns the lack of convenient schools in remote areas, particularly at secondary school level.

Language

As in most other Central and South American countries, the official language of Costa Rica is **Spanish**. Visitors familiar with Spain will find that Costa Rican pronunciation is more akin to Andalucía and the Canary Islands than to Castillian Spanish. Thankfully, however, it is spoken more slowly. As well as the tendency to use diminutives, there are a large number of words used which are typically Costa Rican. *Ticos* always appreciate visitors willing to attempt their language – bring a good phrase book and dictionary.

English is widely spoken in the tourist industry, which caters largely for North American visitors. A form of patois English is also spoken on the Caribbean coast by people of West Indian descent. Some *indigenas* languages still survive in isolated areas of the country, the main one being *Bribrí*, for which an alphabet exists.

Religion

The official religion of Costa Rica is **Roman Catholicism** and some 80 per cent of *ticos* would claim, in principle, to be Catholics. Church festivals are public holidays, but priests often despair at the way Costa Ricans secularize such occasions. Everything closes down during Holy Week, when roads, hotels and beaches are crowded, while banks and shops are closed.

Other religions are tolerated in Costa Rica. The Caribbean blacks are mainly Protestant and there is a small Jewish community in San José. North American Mormons are also slowly gaining a foothold in the country.

INDIGENAS RESERVES

The *indigenas* people of Costa Rica form a mere 1% of the population and most of these are fully integrated into society. The government, however, has decided that their culture should be preserved and in 1977 it set up 22 *indigenas* reserves, mainly in remote areas, such as Talamanca, so that the *indigenas* people can live in self-governing communities. The reserves have very little in the way of infrastructure and have certainly not become tourist attractions.

Above: *The making and painting of traditional ox carts, centred on the village of Sarchí, is Costa Rica's most important craft industry; the designs are thought to have been brought by immigrants from Andalucía in Spain.*
Opposite: *Costa Rica has several top surfing locations, notably on the Pacific coast at Tamarindo and Pavones.*

TOPIARY AT ZARCERO

The mountain village of Zarcero in the northwestern part of the Central Valley has an unusual feature. In the main plaza in front of the village church is an extensive **topiary garden**, the work of landscape gardener Evangelista Blanco. The topiary sculptures are really quite extraordinary and include elephants, church-like vaulting, a bullfighting scene, mythical birds and an ox pulling a cart.

Arts and Crafts

Costa Rica does not have a strong tradition in craft work, probably because of the small number of *indigenas* people remaining. Many souvenir shops are full of craft items, but these have been imported. One finds, for example, textile goods from Guatemala and Panama, woodwork from El Salvador and rocking chairs from Nicaragua. There are some items, however, which are genuinely Costa Rican. Most famous are the brightly painted ox carts (*carretas*) made in the village of Sarchí. The designs are believed to have come from Andalucía and the carts have been scaled down to a size convenient for tourists to take home. Visitors can watch the artisans at work on the ox carts and other items of furniture.

Another genuine Costa Rican craft is the ceramic work which is made in villages in the Nicoya area of Guanacaste province by the Chorotega people. The craft had died out at one time, but was revived after original artefacts were studied at the National Museum at San José. The pottery is characterized by the colourful designs in red and black on a beige background.

Copies of pre-Columbian jewellery in gold and jade can be bought at the museums in San José, along with stone-carved figurines. Some attractive carved wooden items are also available, but environmentally-conscious tourists might wish to ask whether the wood has come from the rain forest or from plantations. Other craft goods on sale include wickerwork, hammocks and leatherwork. Rocking chairs made of wood and leather can fold up for transport home.

Few visitors can resist taking home some Costa Rican coffee. Buy export quality Café Britt, which is available in souvenir shops and hotels. It is possible to buy less expensive coffee at shops and markets, but this will be of lower quality. Purchase whole beans rather than grounds, which may have sugar added.

Sport and Recreation

For Costa Ricans, the word 'sport' means one thing – **football**. Even the smallest village has its football pitch, usually on an open space opposite the church. Larger towns have teams in the two Costa Rican leagues, which play from June to September. This frees star players to perform with distinction in Europe during other times of the year. The Costa Rican national side have qualified for the World Cup in recent years. Other minor spectator sports include **basketball** and **bullfighting**. In the latter, the bull is not killed and the whole event amounts to comic slapstick, with as many as 100 budding toreadors in the ring taunting the bull. For the visitor, there is a wide range of **outdoor activities** to choose from, water sports being extremely popular. Some of the best **surfing** in the world can be experienced along the Pacific coast, especially at Pavones. Equipment can be hired locally. **Snorkelling** and **scuba diving** enthusiasts now have less opportunities since the destruction of much of the coral reef along the Caribbean coast. There is much sea life to observe, but the waters are rarely clear. **Windsurfing** is outstanding at the western end of Lake Arenal, where local hotels have equipment for hire.

BULLFIGHTING, COSTA RICAN STYLE

Aficionados of the Spanish *corrida*, with its strong ritual, will be disappointed with Costa Rican bullfights – **Las Corridas a la Tica**. The bull is not killed and the whole thing is very much a comic event. The bull is taunted and teased by any spectator who cares to jump into the ring – and hundreds do. Most jump out of the ring equally quickly when the bull heads their way, but others will try to trip the bull up or cling to its horns. In San José, there are all-day *corridas* in the suburb of Zapote during the Christmas and New Year holidays.

PAPER FROM WASTE

An enterprising company in Costa Rica has come up with a brilliant idea which is typical of the ecological awareness in the country. The firm obtains unwanted waste paper from neighbouring El Salvador and mixes it with actual brewed coffee and the skins of other beans. The result takes the form of notepads and writing paper. The same firm also uses banana waste in this way. These notepads make great souvenirs for environmentally minded visitors.

RIP TIDES

Many people lose their lives by drowning along Costa Rica's coasts, where there are rarely life guards in attendance. Most of the tragedies are caused by rip tides. Waves break on a broad front, but the water returning to the sea often concentrates into deep, well-defined channels. This returning water is known as a rip tide. If caught in a rip tide, the important thing is **not to panic** or fight against the tide, but drift with the water until it loses its strength. Then **swim parallel to the shore** until the effect of the rip tide diminishes, before swimming back to the beach.

There are many opportunities for **white-water rafting** in Costa Rica. The best known rivers are the Pacuare and the Reventazón. Specialist companies can organize trips from San José and provide all the necessary equipment. There are also local opportunities for **horse riding** and **mountain biking**. Again, specialist firms can provide equipment and give advice on suitable routes. There are good possibilities for **hiking** in many of the National Parks, while for a more challenging trek, head for Mt Chirripó. Some 12 per cent of tourists come to Costa Rica for its world class **sportfishing.** Although the waters are rich in fish, a 'catch and release' policy operates, thereby preserving stocks. There are special fishing lodges where state of the art equipment is provided. Licences are usually part of the package.

Food and Drink

Costa Rican **food** is plain and unpretentious. After a tourist has spent a week or two in the country, it can get monotonous. Nevertheless, it is wholesome and generally includes fresh ingredients, which no doubt contributes to the longevity of *ticos*. A traditional break-fast dish is *gallo pinto* (literally 'spotted rooster'), a colourful mixture of black and red beans, with rice, plus sour cream and fried or scrambled eggs. At lunch and dinner, most restaurants will offer a fish dish (*pescado*) and meat dishes which might be chicken (*pollo*), beef (*bistek*) or pork (*cerdo*). These staple dishes may be served under the name *casado* (literally 'married'), in which case they will come with rice, black beans, *plátano* (fried plantain), chopped cabbage or coleslaw, egg or avocado. There are some interesting

Below: *In several of the country's wetter national parks, rubber boots are an important part of any hiking excursion.*

soups, again featuring the ubiquitous beans. *Sopa negra*, for example, is a black bean soup with a poached egg on top. *Sopa de mondongo*, made with tripe, is an acquired taste. The choice of vegetables is normally limited to cabbage, carrots and mushrooms; salad is often a better bet for freshness and variety. Also on offer in most establishments is *picadillo*, a stewed purée of various vegetables and meat, served as a side dish.

Above: *Enjoy the lively atmosphere of the Central Market in San José, where an amazing range of tropical fruit and fresh vegetables can be found on sale.*

Despite Costa Rica's Pacific and Caribbean coastlines, the choice of seafood is small. *Corvina* (sea bass) is the customary offering. *Atún* (tuna) and *pargo* (red snapper) may also be on the menu, but *langosta* (lobster) is usually prohibitively expensive.

Desserts are many and varied, but nearly always very sweet. A number are based on condensed milk and go under the name of *cajeta*. All menus include *helados* (ice cream) and *flan* (crème caramel). Fortunately, there is a wealth of delicious tropical fruit available, including banana, pawpaw, pineapple, watermelon and mango. Less well-known fruit includes *granadilla* (passion fruit), *carambola* (star fruit) and *marañón* (the fruit of the cashew). Tourists worried about the cleanliness of fruit should stick to the varieties which can be peeled.

There are some regional variations in Costa Rican cooking. In Guanacaste province, for example, corn features prominently in such things as pancakes, stews and doughnuts. On the Caribbean coast, Creole cooking uses a number of African-originated vegetables and spices, coconut and sweet desserts.

THE NATIONAL FLAG

Costa Rica's national flag consists of five vertical stripes coloured blue, white, red, white and blue. *Ticos* will explain that the blue represents the **sky** and the **sea**, the white stands for **peace** with their neighbours to the north and south, while the red represents the **blood** lost in achieving democracy.

BOCAS

Once widespread in Costa Rica, the authentic **boca bar** is fast disappearing. They are now almost entirely confined to urban working class areas, and often have a lively, family atmosphere. **Bocas** are similar to the Spanish tapas – small savoury snacks, offered free or inexpensively as appetizers. Some bars produce a boca menu, but the snacks are usually on display. Typical bocas include *ceviche* (a marinated seafood salad), fried plantains, *gallos* (stuffed tortillas), *tacos*, *tamales* (similar to the Greek dolmades) and *empanadas* (meat or vegetable patties). The perfect accompaniment to a boca is cold beer – but note that even if the snack is free, the beer may be twice the usual price!

Where to Eat

Restaurants open from 11:30 until 14:00 at lunchtime; few stay open after 22:00 in the evening. There is usually a tasty vegetarian option on the menu. Some restaurants are also beginning to set up 'non-smoking' areas. A welcome number of good international restaurants have appeared in Costa Rica in the last decade, particularly in San José, where it is quite easy to find Asian, Italian, French and South American food. Remember that restaurants are obliged to add a total of 23 per cent in taxes to the bill and some do not accept credit cards, especially those out of the city centres.

Visitors on a budget will find that the *sodas* are the cheapest places to eat. Rather like American diners, they usually have a *plato del día* (menu of the day) which will be offered at a bargain price. Many also have take-away windows. American fast food outlets are well established and are popular with *ticos*. Some bars serve *bocas*, which, rather like the Spanish *tapas*, are small savoury dishes designed to make the drink more enjoyable. Formerly free, *bocas* now usually have to be paid for.

Drinks

There are a variety of **drinks** in Costa Rica, but wine lovers will have a hard time. There are no vineyards, so wine is imported and is expensive. The wine generally comes from California or Chile. On the other hand, great local beer is available. Imperial is the most widely sold brand and is identified by the black eagle on the label. Bavaria is slightly more expensive, but has more flavour. Low alcohol and low calorie beers include Tropical and Bavaria Lite. Popular foreign beers now produced here include Heineken, Pilsen and Rock Ice. Imported beers available at supermarkets (but rarely in bars) are Corona, Budweiser, Grolsh, Guiness and Stella Artois. Local spirits made from sugar cane include rum and *guaro* (which is drunk for effect rather than for its flavour). There are also some good Costa Rican liqueurs, such as the coffee flavoured Café Rica.

Costa Rica has some thirst-quenching non-alcoholic drinks, which are generally known as *frescos*. Like a milk shake, they are usually made with fresh fruit and milk. Popular flavours are pineapple, mango and blackberry. In Guanacaste province, a more unusual *fresco* is called *horchata*. Brought originally from Spain, it is made with corn meal and cinnamon. The usual bottled soft drinks, such as lemonade and colas, are also available, where they are known as *refrescos*. Milk is pasteurized and safe to drink.

Water in hotels is usually potable, but you will find that carbonated bottled water (*agua mineral con gas*) is safer, cheap and more refreshing. Coffee is superb and is usually served strong, with a separate jug of hot milk. Some coffee is pre-sweetened. Tea will mainly be of the herbal variety.

**THE HIGHLY
USEFUL COCONUT**

The coconut is commonly found backing the beaches of Costa Rica, and no tree could be more useful. The trunks are used for building and the leaves make an excellent thatching material, but it is the fruit of the coconut which is most valuable. The coir (fibres) are used for matting, while the copra (white fruit) is made into cooking oil and used in confectionery and the preparation of sun cream. Young coconuts or *pipas* are sold on roadside stalls, where they are cut open, the watery milk making a summer drink.

Left: *Similar to Spanish tapas,* bocas *are small savoury snacks; once free with drinks, these appetizers now normally have to be purchased.*

Opposite: *San José has a wide range of international restaurants, including the elegant Café Parisienne, although traditional Costa Rican food is usual in rural areas.*

2
San José

Costa Rica's capital city, San José, was founded in 1737, when it was known as Villa Nueva de la Boca del Monte. In those days it was little more than a few adobe huts around a church. Later, a wealthy coffee bourgeoisie developed, whose affluence ultimately led to the construction of the famous **Teatro Nacional** in 1894.

Today, San José sprawls across the Central Valley at a height of around 1100m (3600ft), containing an estimated 300,000 *josefinos* and nearly a million people in Greater San José. The feel of inner San José is North American, with its filigree of power lines, neon signs and fast food outlets. The majority of the old colonial buildings have been destroyed by the regular **earthquakes** – the last serious one in 1991 did significant damage to both the cathedral and National Theatre. Gridlocked traffic, air pollution and uninspiring architecture leave much to be desired in what is otherwise a country renowned for taking care of its natural environment.

San José does have a number of attractions, which are worth seeking out. The Teatro Nacional should not be missed, while there are a number of good **museums**. Away from the inner city, there are *barrios* such as **Otoya** and **Amón**, which have examples of colonial architecture in leafy boulevards. Further afield, there are attractive **suburbs** such as the university town of **San Pedro**.

Most tourists will probably find one, or at the most, two days enough to devote to San José. It does, however, make an excellent centre for excursions into the Central Valley and has a wide range of accommodation available.

DON'T MISS

*** Teatro Nacional: Baroque masterpiece built by the wealthy coffee barons.
** Gold Museum: largest collection of pre-Columbian gold artefacts and jewellery in Central America.
** Jade Museum: prime exhibition of jade jewellery.
* National Museum: the art, history and archaeology of Costa Rica, displayed in an old army barracks.
* Mercado Central: San José's lively market selling fresh produce and souvenirs.

Opposite: *A busy street in downtown San José; the main shopping section is pedestrianized.*

CLIMATE

San José has an agreeable and healthy climate with few extremes of temperature or rainfall. Temperatures average 20°C (68°F) throughout the year, with the warmest months being April and May. Virtually no rain falls between December and March, but during the wet season it rains frequently, mainly afternoons. Owing to the heavy traffic, the central areas of San José often suffer badly from air pollution.

Opposite: *The interior of the National Theatre, which was commissioned by wealthy coffee barons in the 1890s and constructed by European craftsmen, with no expense spared.*

PLAZA DE LA CULTURA AND AROUND

Most of San José's attractions are located within a small area of the inner city and are generally best seen on foot. Start at the rather uninspiring **Plaza de la Cultura**, which is close to the centre of things and home of the **Tourist Information Office** (ICT), which can provide details of accommodation, restaurants, excursions and brochures about the main attractions in other parts of the country. The west side of the square is home to an open-air artisans market, selling cheap bracelets, souvenir jewellery, hammocks and T-shirts, all at a lower price than in the various craft shops scattered around the city.

Teatro Nacional ★★★

Located on the south side of the Plaza de la Cultura, the National Theatre is undoubtedly San José's most impressive public building. It was built in the 1890s after the opera singer, Adelina Patti, refused to perform in Costa Rica, claiming that there was no suitable venue. After this snub, the coffee barons raised the funds to build a theatre, largely by putting a tax on every bag of their own coffee which was exported. Craftsmen from Europe

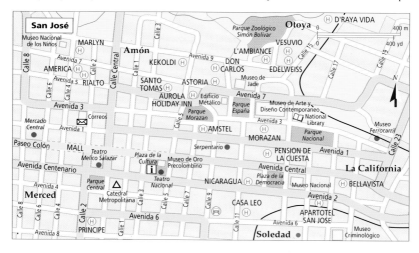

were employed in the construction of the new theatre and no expense was spared. The building is resplendent with marble, gilding, local hardwood and finely detailed glasswork. Look carefully at the ceiling frescos and murals. The largest of the murals appeared on the now defunct five colón note. Others are supposed to depict Costa Rican life at the time, but as they were painted by Italians who had never been to Costa Rica, the scenes are more reminiscent of rural Italy. The magnificent three-storey auditorium is horseshoe-shaped and can house over a thousand people in the original seats. Note the curious concealed boxes on either side of the stage, designed for the widows of the day who preferred not to be seen, but now the home for loudspeakers. Although an earthquake closed the theatre in 1991, it re-opened two years later and celebrated its centenary in 1997. Performances are mainly in the evening. There is a popular coffee shop next to the lobby. Open for guided tours, Monday to Saturday 09:00–17:00.

FINDING AN ADDRESS IN SAN JOSÉ

San José's street pattern is based on a grid plan. **Avenidas** run east-west and **calles** run north-south. Avenida Central and Calle Central bisect the centre of the city. Streets east and north of the centre are odd numbered and streets west and south are even numbered. The confusing result of this is that, for example, Calles 18 and 19 are at opposite ends of the city. Few buildings have a number and the 'address' is based on landmarks. A typical address might be 'Calle 17 Avenida 0/2 (the 0 abbreviating Central), next to the Soda Fernandez'.

SAFETY IN SAN JOSÉ

Although Costa Rica is regarded a safe country, especially by Central American standards, care needs to be taken in central San José, where street crime, such as pickpocketing, is on the increase. A few sensible precautions can prevent a holiday being ruined:
• Leave valuables in the hotel safe. Take a photocopy of the vital pages in your passport.
• If carrying a money belt, conceal it under clothing.
• Avoid unsafe areas and travel by taxi at night.
• Take particular care in crowded parts of the city, such as markets.
• Do not leave any items, especially valuables, in cars.
• Do not park on the street – find a guarded parking lot.

Below: *A fruit seller crosses the Plaza de la Cultura in the city centre.*

Museo de Oro Precolombino ★★

There are a number of museums in San José which are well worth a visit, many located in buildings with rather unusual backgrounds. The Museum of Pre-Columbian Gold is located directly under the Plaza de la Cultura and is owned by the Banco Central. The 2000 gold objects on display are almost entirely the work of the **Diquis** tribe, who lived in the southwest of Costa Rica. They were probably made for the *caciques* and shamans of that time. The majority of the small, but intricate, gold figures represent an unusual variety of animals such as frogs, eagles, spiders and crocodiles. The museum also includes a comprehensive coin and stamp collection. Open Tuesday–Sunday 10:00–17:00.

Central Park ★★

Just west of the Plaza de la Cultura, between Avenida 2 and Calles 2 and 4, is the Central Park. San José has a surprisingly large number of parks and open spaces around its centre, and this landscaped area with its palm trees and bandstand is the most pleasant of them all. Flanked by the cathedral and the Melico Salazar Theatre, it offers several eating possibilities nearby, including the Soda Palace, open 24 hours a day.

The adjacent **Catedral Metropolitana**, which is rather imposing, displays a neoclassical facade. It has survived earthquakes and has had a recent renovation, though the interior boasts no great artworks. It does, however, have a delicately carved wooden ceiling, while the smaller Chapel of the Holy Sacrament is worth a look for its flower theme.

EAST OF THE CITY CENTRE

The first attraction heading east from Plaza de la Cultura is the unusual **Serpentario**, located on the second floor of a building on the corner of Avenida 1 and Calle 9. It has a scary, but well-presented, collection of live snakes, frogs and lizards, with the poisonous snakes the main fascination, especially an enormous Burmese python. Open Monday–Friday 09:00–18:00, weekends 09:00–17:00.

Further east is **Morazan Park**. Though now largely concreted over, this little park has a charming dome-roofed bandstand known as the Temple of Music, numerous statues and a Japanese garden. There is also a children's playground.

Almost next door is another open space, the **Parque España** or Spanish Park. Recently renovated, the tiny park is full of shady trees and has a strange colonial-style pavilion, donated by the National Liquor Factory. There are a number of interesting buildings around the park, including the Jade Museum, the National Cultural Centre and the ochre-coloured **Casa Amarilla** which was once the Court of Justice and is now the Chancellery. One particular curiosity, the **Edificio Metálico**, is a metal building made from steel plates sent over from France early in this century. (The church at Grecia, some 25km northwest of San José, is of similar construction).

Above: *The edge of attractive Parque España is lined by interesting buildings, including the ochre-coloured Casa Amarilla, which now serves as the Chancellery.*

TAXIS IN SAN JOSÉ

San José taxis are red with a yellow triangle on the side. Fares are cheap and officially fixed, but there is a 20% surcharge after 22:00. There may also be a surcharge if a taxi is called from a hotel. When hiring a taxi, make sure that the meter (*maria*) is switched on. There are taxi ranks outside the Teatro Nacional, Parque Central and Parque Nacional. It is not necessary to tip taxi drivers. It is also possible to hire a taxi for half a day or even longer in order to reach parts of the country, such as some of the National Parks.

Above: *San José has an efficient, cheap and well-used bus network which connects to all parts of the suburban area; various companies operate services.*

GAMBLING

Ticos are keen gamblers, and in the absence of horse racing, they head for the casinos, which, with one or two exceptions, are located in the larger hotels, such as the Corobici, Marriot, Cariari, Holiday Inn, Gran Hotel and the Herradura. Visitors will find that some card games, such as blackjack and poker, have *tico* variations. Roulette is played, but the numbers are drawn from numbered balls in a lottery style tumbler, which doesn't quite have the romance of more conventional roulette.

Jade Museum ★★

The Jade Museum can be found on the 11th floor of the Instituto Nacional de Seguros at Avenida 7, Calles 9 and 11. It houses the largest collection of American jade in the world. This durable and much prized mineral, with its variety of colours, has added desirability because of its rarity – there are only six known quarries in the world. The Costa Rican examples probably came from the Motagua valley quarries in Guatemala, as some of the items feature Maya symbols. Cleverly lit and displayed in the museum, these pre-Columbian artefacts mainly take the form of amulets and pendants, representing animals or as intricate geometric patterns, while one whole room is devoted to male fertility symbols. The museum is open Monday–Friday 08:00–16:30. The view from the windows over the city of San José and beyond to the mountains is truly stunning.

National Park

Located at the eastern end of the inner city area, this shady park has two statues of note. Right in the centre of the park is the National Monument to those nations which drove William Walker out of Central America, while in the southwest corner is a statue of Juan Santamaría. The Square has a number of important buildings around it, including the Legislative Assembly and the **Biblioteca Nacional** (National Library), housed in a large modern building. Nearby is the **Museo de Arte y Diseño Contemporaneo** (Modern Art and Design Museum), which is located in the old National Liquor Factory and features work by Costa Rican artists. Open Monday–Saturday 10:00–13:00 and 14:00–17:00.

Railway Museum and National Museum *

Beyond the National Park is the **Museo Ferrocarril** (Railway Museum), housed in the Estación Atlántico terminus of the old 'Jungle Train'. Trains formerly ran from here to Puerto Limón, until the earthquake in 1991 closed the line. The mainly photographic memorabilia on display will appeal to railway enthusiasts. Open Monday–Thursday 09:00–16:00, Friday 09:00–15:30.

South of the Railway Museum, on the rather sterile Plaza de la Democracia, is the **Museo Nacional** (National Museum). The museum occupies the old Bellavista army barracks, where on the south wall the more curious visitor can spot bullet holes dating from the 1948 Civil War. Inside, there is a superb archaeology section with artefacts of gold and jade, and *metates* or grinding stones, while in the courtyard there are some of the lithic spheres from the southwest of the country and a collection of herbal plants. The history section gives a graphic account of the virtual extinction of the *indigenas* people, along with pieces of religious art from the colonial period. In another section, cardboard cut-out figures demonstrate the racial and ethnic origins of modern Costa Ricans. Outside the building, there is a collection of some of Costa Rica's common trees and shrubs. This is another spot from where there are wonderful views over the city. Open Tuesday–Saturday 08:30–17:00, Sunday 09:00–17:00.

> ### THE B AND B PHENOMENON
>
> One of the more interesting developments in tourism in Costa Rica during the 1990s has been the growth of establishments offering bed and breakfast. Some are traditional inns, but more often they are houses of character converted by foreigners in one of the more peaceful areas of San José. Some Costa Rican families are now offering bed and breakfast – a good way of getting to know *ticos* in their home environment.

Below: *Located on the 11th floor of an office block, the Jade Museum is one of San José's top attractions, with magnificent artefacts and an equally impressive view over the city.*

The aim of this macabre museum is to deter visitors from taking up a life of crime. It is hard to imagine it having any other effect. There are gory photographs, murder weapons, pickled parts of dismembered bodies and displays showing the history of law and punishment in Costa Rica. The museum is in the Courts of Justice, Avenida 6 and 8, Calle 17. Open 13:00–16:00, Mondays, Wednesdays and Fridays.

Below: *The commercial centre of San Pedro has food outlets and nightclubs.*

NORTH AND EASTERN SUBURBS

Most *josefinos* live in the suburbs, which are full of open spaces and trees, particularly the stunning *Erythina*, whose golden blossom is a feature of the dry season. Many of the poorer inner city suburbs should be avoided by the visitor, but there are several notable exceptions.

Amón and Otoya ★

These two *barrios* to the northeast of the inner city are full of 19th-century buildings built by the coffee barons, then neglected, but recently rediscovered and gentrified. In the vicinity is the **Museo de los Niños** (Children's Museum), housed in a former prison. It has a hi-tech approach, with plenty of 'hands-on' opportunities. There is a good section on the historical development of Costa Rica, while few children will want to miss the simulated earthquake. Open Tuesday–Sunday 09:00–12:00 and 14:00–17:00. Also in the northern suburbs is the **Spirogyra Jardín de Mariposas**, located close to the large shopping mall Centro Comercial El Pueblo. A small yet fascinating butterfly farm, it offers bilingual tours every 30 minutes. Open daily 09:00–17:00.

San Pedro ★

Heading east from Avenida Central is the pleasant suburb of San Pedro. On the way are the *barrios* of **La California** and **Los Yoses** which, like Amón and Otoya, are favoured by foreign embassies. **San Pedro** itself is the home of the University of Costa Rica, whose campus must be the most impressive in Central America. San Pedro has some excellent bookshops, a huge open air theatre, stately old houses and some of the finest bars, restaurants and nightclubs in the city.

In keeping with San José's other museums, San Pedro has its own oddly located museum. The **Museo de Entomología** (Insect Museum) is found in the basement of the University's School of Music. Over a million insects are displayed, of which the butterflies have the main appeal. Open Monday–Friday 13:00–16:00.

SABANA PARK AND ESCAZÚ

To the west of the inner city, Sabana Park occupies the site of the old airfield. The former terminal building is now the Museum of Costa Rican Art, while in the south-west corner there is the Natural Science Museum. La Sabana has excellent sports facilities, including tennis courts, volleyball and basketball. There is also a network of jogging paths. The **Museo de Arte Costarricense** (Museum of Costa Rican Art) concentrates on 20th-century national painters. The second floor has some impressive bas-relief murals by a French artist showing idealized scenes from Costa Rica's history, from pre-Columbian times right through to the present. Open Tuesday–Sunday 10:00–16:30. The **Museo de Ciencias Naturales** is located in the former La Salle high school near Sabana Park. It consists of a collection of stuffed animals, birds, pinned butterflies and fossils. Open Monday–Friday 08:00–16:00, Saturday 08:00–12:00, Sunday 09:00–16:00.

Escazú

Further out, on the higher land to the west, is the suburb of **Escazú**, with several excellent hotels. It is a fashionable residential area which is popular with foreign residents. The central area of Escazú has some adobe buildings and an interesting church, while there are a number of American-style shopping malls.

Above: *Near to Sabana Park is the comfortable Hotel Grano de Oro.*

CENTRO COMERCIAL EL PUEBLO

Of all the shopping malls which have developed in San José in recent years, Centro Comercial El Pueblo is by far the most interesting. Located just north of the Simón Bolívar Zoo, it is built in traditional style with adobe buildings, winding alleyways and small squares. Possibly much of Costa Rica would have been like this, but for the frequent earthquakes. There are numerous shops, many selling souvenirs, though mostly at higher prices than in the downtown shops of San José. The many discos, bars and night-clubs ensure that El Pueblo is just as popular at night time as during the day.

San José at a Glance

San José is an all-year-round destination, with an agreeable climate. During the wet season, the rain rarely lasts long and is usually confined to the afternoon. Avoid Easter when the city closes down. On the other hand Christmas and New Year are enjoyable with a carnival, parades bullfights and fiestas.

Most visitors arrive through San José's **Juan Santamaría Airport,** which has a new modern terminal with much improved baggage handling and air conditioning. The airport is located near **Alajuela,** 17km (10 miles) from the city. **Domestic flights** also use this airport, along with the smaller **Pavas Airport** closer to the city. Airport **taxis** are orange in colour and will take 20–30 minutes to reach downtown San José. Service **buses** also run from Alajuela to San José, stopping at the airport *en route,* taking 30–35 minutes to reach the city centre.

The inner city sights are close together and best visited on foot. There are over 3000 **taxis** in San José, so finding one is not usually a problem except during the rush hour. Fares are cheap and drivers are obliged by law to use their meters (although few do – it is best to negotiate the fare before moving off). Expect to pay a surcharge at night. San José has an excellent **bus** network with very cheap fares. Buses can be crowded during the rush hours. There are frequent bus stops or *paradas,* but not all buses stop at each one. The ICT has a current list of bus timetables. Buses should have the company name, route number and destination on the windscreen.

San José has a full range of accommodation to fit every pocket and taste.

LUXURY
Hotel Herradura, Apdo.7-1800, San José 1007, tel: 239-0033, fax: 239-2292. Near airport, pools and spa, casino, choice of 4 restaurants.
Hotel Corobicí, Apdo.2443, San José 1000, tel: 232-8122, fax: 231-5834. Near Sabana Park, huge atrium, spa, casino and 2 restaurants.
Hotel Aurola Holiday Inn, Apdo.7802, San José 1000, tel: 233-7233, fax: 255-1036. Best downtown hotel. Gym, pool, 17th-floor restaurant.
Costa Rica Marriot, La Ribera de Belén, tel: 298-0000, fax: 298-8998. Between airport and downtown San José. Pools, health club and restaurants.
MID-RANGE
Hotel Grano de Oro, Apdo.1157, San José 1007, tel: 255-3322, fax: 221-2782. Outstanding boutique hotel in quiet neighbourhood. Superb restaurant for all tastes.
Hotel Bougainvillea, Apdo.69-2120, San José, tel: 240-1414, fax: 240-1313. Outskirts of town, tennis, pool, shuttle bus to city centre.
Hotel Milvia, Apdo.1660, San Pedro 2050,tel: 225-4543, fax: 225-7801. Boutique hotel in Caribbean-style wooden house.
BUDGET
Pensión de la Cuesta, Avenida 1, Calles 11/13, tel: 255-2896, fax: 223-6808. House owned by local artists.
Hotel Edelweiss, Avenida 9, Calle 13/15, Barrio Otoya, San José, tel: 221-9702, fax: 222-1241. In good downtown area, near the museums and the National Theatre.
Hotel Vesuvio, Avenida 11, Calles 13/15, tel: 221-7586, fax: 221-8325. Quiet location, TV in rooms, restaurant.

There are a range of restaurants in San José. The cheapest places are downtown in the *sodas* and snack bars, while the more expensive options are in the more affluent suburbs. Many hotels have excellent restaurants. Remember that there is a 23% tax on meals (10% service, 13% sales tax) and payment by credit card may attract a further fee.

LUXURY
Ambrosia, near Banco Popular, San Pedro, tel: 253-8012. International cuisine and a cosy atmosphere.

San José at a Glance

Le Chandelier, near the ICE Building, San Pedro, tel: 225-3980. Exclusive French food.
L'Ile de France, Calle 7, Avenida Central/2, tel: 222-4241. Classic French restaurant in downtown location.
Cerutti, near the crossroads of San Rafael de Escazú, tel: 228-4511. A range of Italian dishes in nice atmosphere.
MID-RANGE
Café Mundo, Avenida 9, Calle 15, tel: 222-6190. International dishes in a casual atmosphere.
Antojitos, West of Sabana Park, tel: 231-5564. Authentic Mexican cuisine with live music at weekends.
El Fogón de Leña, El Pueblo Shopping Centre, tel: 233-9964. High quality *tico* food in mock farmhouse.
Machu Picchu, Calle 38 125m N of Paseo Colón, tel: 222-7384. Experience genuine South American food.
Restaurant Lukas, El Pueblo Shopping Centre, tel: 233-8145. Costa Rican food with open air grill and live jazz.
Tin-Jo, Calle 11, Avenidas 6/8, tel: 221-7605. Thai and Burmese food, excellent service.
BUDGET
Sodas are the cheapest option, particularly at lunch, when a *plata del día* is usually offered.
Pollo Campesino, Calle 7, Avenidas 2/4. Wood-roasted chicken is the speciality of this restaurant.
Vishnu, Avenida 1, Calles 3/5. Well-established and popular vegetarian restaurant.

SHOPPING

The main shopping street in San José is the pedestrianized section of Avenida Central, which has department stores, book shops and other specialist outlets. The shops spill out into Avenidas 1 and 2. For cheap fresh fruit and vegetables, go to the Mercado Central. In the suburbs, basics can be obtained from the stores or *pulperías*. There are shops selling arts and crafts in the Centro Comercial El Pueblo in the north of the inner city. Find other craft outlets in the suburb of Moravia.

TOURS AND EXCURSIONS

San José is a good centre for day trips in to the Central Valley and surrounding highlands. The top sights are the many volcanoes. The three most popular are Volcán Arenal, Volcán Irazú and Volcán Poás. The last two have parking areas a short walk from their craters. Tours to the Orosí Valley are often combined with a visit to the Lankester Botanical Gardens. Many of the National Parks and Reserves are within reach of San José, including Braulio Carrillo, Tapantí and the Monteverde Cloud Forest.

USEFUL CONTACTS

Instituto Costarricense de Turismo (ICT). Located below the Plaza de la Cultura, Avenida Central, Calle 3-5, tel: 222-1090. It can supply accommodation details, city plans, maps and bus schedules.
National Parks' Office (SPN), Avenidas 8-10, Calle 25, tel: 257-0922, fax: 223-6963. The SPN provides information on the national parks, free maps and offers passes which work out cheaper than buying a ticket. Reliable tour operators in Costa Rica include:
TAM Travel, Avenida 1, Calles 1-3, tel: 222-3866. Professional organization for the upper end of the market.
Camino Travel, Avenida 0-1, Calle 1, tel: 257-0107 or 234-2530, fax: 225-6143. An enthusiastic group, specializing in tailor-made tours for both groups and individuals.
Costa Rica Expeditions, Calle Central, Avenida 3, tel: 257-0766. Established firm with excellent accommodation in wildlife locations. For internal domestic flights:
SANSA, Calle 24, Paseo Colón, tel: 221-9414.
Travelair, Tobias Bolaños Airport, tel: 232-7883.

SAN JOSÉ	J	F	M	A	M	J	J	A	S	O	N	D
AVERAGE TEMP. °F	66	66	68	70	70	70	69	69	69	69	68	67
AVERAGE TEMP. °C	19	19	20	21.5	21.5	21.5	21	21	21	20.5	20	19.5
RAINFALL in	0.3	0.2	0.4	1.5	9.6	11.2	9.1	9.2	13.5	13.1	6.8	1.8
RAINFALL mm	8	5	10	37	244	284	230	233	342	333	172	46

3
The Central Valley and Surrounding Highlands

Although widely referred to as the **Valle Central**, this area is an undulating upland area between 1000m (3300ft) and 3000m (9800ft) above sea level, surrounded by volcanic mountains. To the north and east is the **Cordillera Central**, with the active volcanoes Poás and Irazú. To the south is the start of the **Cordillera de Talamanca**, while to the west is the lower lying **Fila de Bustamente**, before the land drops down to the Pacific coastal plain.

Over 60 per cent of the country's population lives here. This includes a number of foreigners, attracted partly by the favourable climate. The National Geographic Society once concluded that two towns in the province – La Garita and Atenas – 'had the best climate in the world'. This region is the location of three provincial capitals, **Alajuela**, **Cartago** and **Heredia**, plus a host of attractive smaller towns and villages. Despite the tourist potential of the area, none of the provincial capitals are geared up for visitors and none has a tourist information office!

The fertility of the area's soil ensures that agriculture is the main form of employment. In Alajuela, fruit such as mangoes and strawberries dominate. Further east, in Heredia and Cartago provinces, coffee is king. On the higher, wetter land, herds of Holstein cattle provide the bulk of the country's milk and cheese.

Despite the dense population, the quality of the road network remains varied. There are a few stretches of dual carriageway leading out of San José, but after this the roads become narrow, winding and badly signposted.

DON'T MISS

*** Rain Forest Aerial Tram: chair lift ride through the canopy near Braulio Carrillo.
*** Poás Volcano: walk up to the rim of the crater.
** Irazú Volcano: evocative lunar-type landscape.
** Sarchí Village: craft shops specialising in traditionally painted ox carts.
* Lankester Botanical Gardens: 800 orchid species.
* Guayabo: pre-Columbian archaeological site.
* Butterfly Farms: three to choose from in the Valley.

Opposite: *The church at Sarchí features a traditional ox cart wheel on one of its towers.*

CLIMATE

With one of the most pleasant climates in the world, the Central Valley has an average **temperature** of 20°C (68°F) throughout the year. **Rain** falls in the wet season from June to October, when showers can be heavy. The surrounding mountains and volcanoes are always much cooler and often covered in cloud.

Opposite: *The church at Grecia is made of steel plates imported from Belgium, a material that has proved highly effective at resisting earthquake shock waves.*

ALAJUELA AND AROUND

Located 18km (11 miles) northwest of San José, the city of Alajuela is close to the country's main airport and many travellers prefer to stop here overnight before catching their flight, rather than staying in San José. Alajuela and its suburbs have a population of just over 170,000, making it the second largest city in the country. Although founded in 1657, little architecture from this period remains, due to earthquake damage. Today it is largely an agricultural town, with a bustling Saturday market well supported by locals.

Alajuela's main claim to fame is the fact that it was the birthplace and home of **Juan Santamaría**, the national hero in the fight against William Walker in 1856. In the middle of the city is the shady **Central Park**, with a pretty, domed bandstand and resident sloths in its trees. The park is gracefully surrounded by buildings from the 19th century, including the gleaming white **cathedral**, with its two towers, classical facade and red corrugated iron roof. Inside are the cathedral tombs where two former presidents rest – Tomás Guardia and León Cortés Castro.

Further to the east is the rather more attractive Baroque-style **Iglesia La Agonía**, with a bright interior containing some unusual modern murals. To the south is the leafy **Juan Santamaría Park**, dominated by the imposing statue of Costa Rica's national hero.

The other feature of note in Alajuela is the fascinating **Juan Santamaría Cultural-Historical Museum**, located close to Central Park and housed, rather appropriately, in an old colonial jail. This museum tells the story of

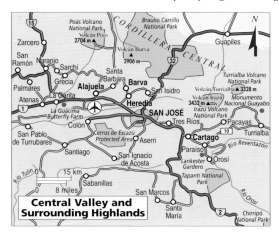

Central Valley and Surrounding Highlands

the war against the American filibuster William Walker, with maps, paintings and other momentos from that period of Costa Rica's history.

There are a number of attractive excursion possibilities around Alajuela. To the south of town are two **'water parks'**, the Ojo de Agua and the more up-market Acua Mania, both with a wide range of recreational activities. Visitors with biological interests will be attracted to **La Guácima**, one of the better butterfly farms in Costa Rica, and **Zoo-Ave**, which claims to be the largest aviary in Central America. Zoo-Ave is located to the west of Alajuela, near the town of La Garita and is a marvellous place to identify some of Costa Rica's many birds. The birds are well kept and many are free flying. There are also mammals, such as monkeys and racoons, again in spacious pens. Open daily 09:00–16:30.

NATIONAL HERO

Juan Santamaría was a young drummer boy who distinguished himself in the fight against William Walker, the American filibuster, in the battle at Rivas in Nicaragua in 1856. Santamaría volunteered to torch the fortress which Walker's men were defending. He succeeded and the battle was won, but he died in a hail of bullets. He is commemorated with a statue in a park in Alajuela, which also has a museum devoted to artefacts from the war. (Open Tuesday–Sunday 10:00–18:00).

Surrounding Villages

The roads leading northwest from Alajuela pass through a number of attractive villages, some worth stopping at. **Grecia** is notable for its steel church and the fact that is the only bungee jumping location in the whole of Costa Rica. **Palmares** is best known for its annual fiesta held in mid-January. The small town of **San Ramón** is remarkable for the number of Presidents and other Costa Ricans of note who have hailed from here, all of whom are celebrated in the local museum.

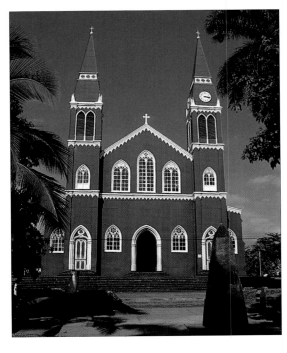

THE CHURCH AT GRECIA

Grecia's distinctive crimson-coloured church is actually made of steel plates riveted together, a building material which is effective against earthquakes. The plates were made in Belgium and should have been sent to Punta Arenas in southern Chile, but somehow they ended up at Puntarenas on the Pacific coast of Costa Rica. There they remained for some time, before someone could be found to piece the plates together and construct the church, replacing one earlier destroyed by an earthquake at Grecia.

Below: *A craftsman decorates pottery in the artisan village of Sarchí.*
Opposite: *The attractive Botos Lake, a 20-minute walk from the summit of Volcán Poás, occupies the site of a former crater.*

The most visited village in Alajuela province, however, is undoubtedly **Sarchí**, Costa Rica's prime craft centre. Shops and craft factories line the main street in the south of the village and it is possible for visitors to watch artisans at work in the larger establishments. The most common craft item is the gaudily painted ox cart, which comes in various sizes from table-top to full-scale. The painted designs are reputed to have come from Andalucía with early Spanish settlers and are probably Moorish in origin. The rear garden of the largest of the craft factories has displays of full-size carts, some of which are pulled around by pairs of oxen. Other items on sale include wooden bowls, leather rocking chairs, practical hammocks and the ubiquitous T-shirts. Firms will freight larger items to visitors' home addresses. The less commercialized, but rarely visited, northern part of Sarchí is surprisingly attractive, with a pretty pink-and-turquoise-coloured church. Fittingly, there is an ox cart wheel on the top of one of the towers.

Volcán Poás ★★★

The most popular excursion in Alajuela province for both tourists and *ticos* alike is to **Volcán Poás**. Surrounded by its own protective National Park, Poás is certainly one of the most accessible volcanoes in the world. A road leads to a car park, from where it is a gentle 200m walk to the rim of the crater. Poás, which is 2704m (8000ft) high, last had a minor eruption in 1989, but brief gas emissions or other activity can temporarily close the park to the public, as happened in 1994. The crater, claimed to be one of the largest in the world, is about 1500m (1 mile) wide, with a

bewitching turquoise-coloured crater lake, through which gas, steam and the occasional sudden geyser spew. A 20-minute walk from the crater rim leads to an extinct side crater with another colourful stretch of water, the Botos Lake. The upper slopes of Poás are covered with dwarf cloud forest, stunted by the cold, the ash and acid rain emissions. The slopes contain unusual wildlife, including the small indigenous Poás squirrel and the sparrow-like volcano junco. There is a visitor centre, with café and gift shop, audio visual show and a mildly interesting insect museum. It is best to visit Poás early in the morning, as by about 11:00 it is usually cloud covered.

On the eastern flanks of Poás, just outside the Park boundary, is the frequently photographed and much visited **Cascada La Paz** (Peace Waterfall). About 8km (5 miles) north of the village of Vara Blanca, it makes a delightful diversion. The Peace Waterfall can easily be viewed from the road, though the adventurous at heart can also walk behind the curtain of falling water.

BUTTERFLY FARMS

Butterflies (*mariposas*) are abundant all over Costa Rica, where it is estimated that 10% of the world's species can be found. One National Park claims to have recorded 3000 species of butterflies and moths. A number of butterfly farms have been established in the country and pupae are now exported all over the world. Many of the farms are open to the public and there are some popular ones in the Central Valley, including **Spirogyra Jardín de Mariposas** in San José and **La Guácima**, close to Alajuela. Both farms have free-flying butterflies in tropical gardens and guides to describe the complex butterfly life cycle.

COFFEE FARM VISITS

Coffee is now Costa Rica's most important export and the country's biggest producer is **Café Britt**. One of the most popular excursions from San José is a 'coffee tour' to the Café Britt *finca*. An audio visual presentation describes the historical importance of coffee to Costa Rica and this is followed by a tour to observe the production processes. The visit is completed by coffee tasting. Combine the excursion with a visit to Volcán Poás or to a butterfly farm.

HEREDIA

Capital of the province of the same name, this small city of 75,000 inhabitants has more of a colonial air than any other Costa Rican town. Situated some 11km (7 miles) north of San José, on the lower slopes of Volcán Barva, Heredia was founded in 1706 and has a number of historic buildings which have survived the earthquakes, including its main church, the **Basilica de la Inmaculada Concepción**. It was dedicated in 1763 and has remained in use ever since, largely thanks to its sturdy, thick-pillared design (generally known as 'seismic Baroque'). There is little of interest or great beauty in the interior, although the Madonna with her neon halo exerts a certain graceless fascination.

Nearby, alongside the shady **Central Park**, is the **El Fortín** tower – all that remains of an old Spanish fortress. On the opposite side of the Calle Central is the **Casa de la Cultura**, based in a stately old colonial house with a typically wide veranda and once the home of a former President. Although there are no other monuments of interest, a stroll around the narrow streets with their adobe buildings is a rewarding experience. The **Universidad Nacional** is located on the eastern edge of Heredia and has a notable Marine Zoological Museum, while on the western side is the football stadium, home of Costa Rica's top team.

Around Heredia

The countryside around Heredia is intensely farmed and largely given over to coffee plantations. Some of the coffee *fincas* can be visited on half-day trips. There is a coffee research station at San Pedro and a number of pleasant small towns and villages close to Heredia. Just 2km (1 mile) north of the city is the colonial village of **Barva**. The settlement dates back to 1561, although most of today's buildings are 18th-century, including the large Baroque church. The whole village is classed as a National Historic Monument. East of Heredia is the craft village of **Moravia**, with several shops selling the usual carved wooden goods, model ox carts, leather work, ceramics and jewellery. One shop specializes in the work of the Bribrí indigenous tribe. South of Heredia is the village of **Santo**

Domingo, where the newly opened Museo Joyas del Trópico Húmedo shows a vast collection of insects from the rain forest. **Monte de la Cruz** and **San José de la Montaña** are attractive mountain villages with various small hotels and restaurants. For villages with attractive churches, head to **San Joaquín de Heredia**, which has a vibrant Easter week procession, and **Santa Barbara**. East of Heredia is a group of villages which go under the collective name of **Coronado** and have a popular festival in May. The main attraction here is the Snake Farm, run by the University of Costa Rica and open to the public. At certain times visitors can observe the snakes being milked for their venom, which is then used in the production of antivenin, and also watch the animals gobbling live mice at feeding time.

SONGBIRD FRIENDLY COFFEE

In the early days of coffee growing, it was necessary to grow **shade trees** at intervals, but new strains of coffee have been developed which make these unnecessary. This has had the effect of reducing the habitat of North American songbirds which spend the winter in Costa Rica. Environmentalists campaigned for a return of the shade trees and it is now possible to buy 'songbird friendly coffee' produced by the old methods.

Above: *Affluent Barva is classed as a National Historic Monument.*
Below: *A local bus halts outside Barva's 18th-century Baroque church.*
Opposite: *The unusual gunports of El Fortín Tower widen on the outside.*

Above: *The aerial tram near Braulio Carrillo takes visitors through the canopy.*

THE RAIN FOREST AERIAL TRAM

One problem of observing wildlife in the rain forest is that the majority of species live in the canopy far above the forest floor. This problem is solved by the **aerial tram** which operates on private property bordering the Braulio Carrillo National Park. Brainchild of American biologist **Donald Perry**, it consists of 22 open-sided, overhead cable cars, each taking five passengers and a naturalist guide, following a 2.6km (1.6 miles) course at canopy and other levels. It was constructed with minimum disturbance as most of the material was brought in on foot. The tram is not cheap, but, for many people it will be the highlight of their visit to Costa Rica.

BRAULIO CARRILLO NATIONAL PARK ★★★

When it was decided to construct a new highway from San José to Puerto Limón on the Caribbean coast via Guápiles, environmentalists were concerned that the virgin rain and cloud forest on the eastern watershed of the Central Valley would be under threat. In 1978 it was therefore decided to set up the Braulio Carrillo National Park, named after one of the country's 19th-century presidents. Covering some 46,000ha (113,700 acres), the prized park includes a range of five altitudinal life zones and holds a tremendous variety of flora and fauna. The new highway effectively cuts the park in two, but gives an excellent opportunity to view the vegetation while travelling by. At one stage there are vast roadside tracts of *gunnera*, which, with its massive leaves, is known as 'the poor man's umbrella'. The main entrance to the park is on the south side of the highway, where there is a small car park. A tractor truck then takes visitors to the reception centre, where there is a video presentation, followed by a trip on the Aerial Tram. Early morning visitors should see a wide range of bird life, with the possibility of seeing the resplendent quetzal. Butterflies are found in profusion, including the stunning blue morpho.

Also in the Braulio Carrillo National Park is **Volcán Barva,** which rises to 2906m (9534ft). Less accessible than some of the other volcanoes, Barva can only be climbed on foot. Various trails lead to the summit, which has several crater lakes. Some of the trails are poorly maintained, however, so advice from the park rangers should be obtained before setting out.

CARTAGO AND AROUND

Some 21km (13 miles) from San José and1438m (4700ft) above sea level, Cartago, founded in 1563, was for three hundred years the capital of Costa Rica. Despite its ancient origins, there are few buildings of historic value left in Cartago today, due to the depredations of earthquakes, volcanic mud slides and floods. Today, Cartago has a population of around 120,000 and is a busy market town with an increasing amount of peripheral industry.

There is an attractive **Central Park**, to the east of which are **Las Ruinas**, the remains of an unfinished church which was destroyed by an earthquake in 1910 and never restored. Five minutes walk to the east is Cartago's other main attraction, the **Basilica de Nuestra Señora de los Angeles**. The original cathedral was destroyed in the 1926 earthquake and rebuilt in Byzantine style. The imposing blue and white exterior is matched by the all-wooden interior, with its paint and gilt work and attractive stained glass windows. The basilica is the home of *La Negrita*, the Black Madonna and patron saint of Costa Rica. This 20cm (8in) black statue sits in splendour in a shrine which forms part of the main altar. Legend has it that the holy image was discovered on the spot by a small girl in 1635. Each time she took it away, the statue miraculously returned to the site. Now every year on 2 August pilgrims come on foot in pilgrimage all the way from San José, traditionally shuffling the last part of the route on their knees. A chapel to the left of the altar displays an extraordinary collection of ex-votos from pilgrims who claim to have been cured by La Negrita.

THE NATIONAL BIRD

It is curious that a country which has exotic birds such as the quetzal, scarlet macaw, hummingbird and parrot, should choose as its national bird a rather drab, brown species called the **clay-coloured robin**. The robin does not even sing very often, confining its trilling to April. This month, however, is the start of the rainy season and the beginning of the fresh agricultural cycle, so the robin's song is a significant time marker.

Below: *The Basilica de Nuestra Señora de los Angeles in Cartago is home to the statue of the Black Madonna, the patron saint of Costa Rica; the cathedral was rebuilt after the earthquake of 1926.*

THE HOUSE OF THE DREAMER

An off-beat place to visit in the Orosí Valley, near the Cachí reservoir, is the **Casa del Soñador** or Dreamer's House. It was built by the late **Macedonio Quesada**, a well-known Costa Rican woodcarver. The exterior is mainly constructed of bamboo, while the interior is full of coffee wood carvings of life-size figures, some of a religious nature, others of farmworkers. Quesada died in 1995, but his sons carry on the tradition. Some items are offered for sale to the public.

Below: *The Orosí Valley is a popular tourist excursion from San José, with its lake, ruined villages, attractive botanical gardens and various fine restaurants.*

Orosí Valley

The area to the southeast of Cartago is one of the most attractive parts of the Central Valley. Just past the village of Paraíso are the **Lankester Gardens**, where orchids are the main attraction. Some 800 species are displayed here. They were originally the private collection of an English biologist, Charles Lankester, but the Gardens are now administered by the University of Costa Rica. The best time to visit is between February and April, when the blooms are at their best, but there will be something in flower throughout the year. The delightfully unkempt 'gardens' are, in fact, a series of trails through tropical pre-montane forest, with trees festooned with epiphytes and lianas. A variety of other plants and flowers can be seen, including ferns and palms, plus a special cacti display. The vegetation in turn attracts birds and butterflies in abundance. Open 08:30–15:30 daily, but closed on national holidays.

East of the Lankester Gardens the road leads into the attractive **Orosí Valley**, in the centre of which is Lake Cachí, formed by the damming of the upper reaches of the Reventazón river. One branch of the road leads to the ruined settlement of **Ujarras**, while the other branch leads to the village of Orosí, which boasts the oldest

surviving church in Costa Rica. The **Church of San José de Orosí** dates from 1743 and should be on every visitor's itinerary. It was probably built by Franciscan monks and the remains of their monastery can be seen alongside. The church is a simple affair with a low-slung tiled roof, adobe walls and a detached bell tower. Inside, the wooden roof, ornate altar and simple wooden pews are admirable, and there is a curious wooden balcony over the entrance door. Oil paintings of the stations of Christ's cross line the walls of the aisles. Attached to the church is a small **Museum of Religious Art**, housed in the former monastery buildings. Nearby are a couple of relaxing thermal pools, which are popular with *ticos* at weekends.

At the end of the Orosí Valley, the northern slopes of Cordillera de Talamanca become apparent, marked by the little visited **Tapantí National Park**. Its forested slopes are reputed to receive up to 7000mm (280in) of rain annually. Despite this, the short trails (one of which leads to a mirador) are popular with bird watchers and over 200 species have been recorded here, including a selection of parrots, hummingbirds, toucans, and even the quetzal. There are plenty of mammals, including jaguar, ocelot and agouti. The dry season is the best time to visit, although even then it is likely to be more wet than dry.

Above: *Over 800 species of orchid are displayed at Lankester Gardens: given to the nation by an English biologist, the gardens are now administered by the University of Costa Rica.*

UJARRAS

Eleven kilometres (7 miles) east of Paraíso is the abandoned village of **Ujarras**, with the ruined church of **Nuestra Señora de la Limpia Concepción**. The church goes back to 1681 and was built on the site of a shrine to the Virgin, who revealed herself in a tree to a local fisherman. The villagers finally abandoned the area in 1833 after a series of floods. Today, the grounds around the church are beautifully cared for and are the venue for a procession from Paraíso each April.

Above: *Visitors can drive to the summit of Volcán Irazú and look down into the complex of craters, one of which is filled with a pea-green coloured lake; the volcano last erupted in 1963.*

Volcán Irazú ★★

A popular excursion near to Cartago is to **Volcán Irazú**, with a spectacular drive to the summit through fields of coffee, potatoes and other crops grown on the fertile volcanic soil. Set in its own national park, the volcano rises to 3432m (11,260ft) and its summit has a complex of four craters, surrounded by swathes of dramatic volcanic ash. The Diego de la Haya crater has a lake which is pea-green in colour, while the larger adjacent crater is some 300m (1080ft) deep. Another nearby crater is wide and shallow and covered with black volcanic ash, inviting comparisons with the surface of the moon.

Volcán Irazú last erupted on 19 March 1963, the day when US President John F. Kennedy visited the country, depositing a thick layer of ash and rocks on the surrounding area. Since then it has been fairly quiet, with a little fumerole activity now and then. The craters can be reached easily along a short path from the car park. Good visibility is essential for a visit to Irazú. It is sometimes possible to see both the Caribbean Sea and the Pacific Ocean on a clear, bright day, but more usually the summit is cloud-covered and cold, so be sure to take warm and protective clothing.

LIVING FENCES

Wherever there are cattle in Costa Rica, the pasture land is contained by living fences. These are in fact the saplings of certain types of tree, spaced at regular distances, cut to a level height and joined by wire. Some of the trees are allowed to grow to their full height to provide shade for the cattle.

TURRIALBA

This small town 45km (28 miles) east of Cartago was once an important stopping place on the San José to Puerto Limón road, but since the new highway via Guápiles was constructed and the Jungle railway line closed, it has become something of a backwater. It is still an important agricultural town, but the small number of tourists who visit Turrialba tend to come for the white-water rafting on the Reventazón, Turrialba and Pacuaré rivers. The local **Volcán Turrialba** is currently dormant, but is rarely visited, except on horseback tours.

Monumento Nacional Guayabo *

A mere 19km (12 miles) northeast of Turrialba is the Guayabo pre-Columbian archaeological site. While not comparable with the Mayan and Aztec sites further north in Central America, it is nevertheless of im-portance. It was discovered by an explorer and naturalist, Anastasio Alfaro, in the late 1800s, though it was not until 1968 that the first serious systematic excavations began.

C.A.T.I.E.

Keen gardeners will certainly want to visit the *Centro Agrónomo Tropical de Investigación y Enseñanza* (C.A.T.I.E.). Located 5km (3 miles) southeast of Turrialba on the road to Siquerres, it is one of the world's most important centres for research into the development of tropical agriculture. Coffee and cacao research dominates, but there is a wide variety of ornamental plants grown in addition. Open for guided tours Monday–Friday 08:00–16:00.

Below: *Though no longer permitted, it was previously possible to walk along the ridge of the main crater of Volcán Irazú.*

Above: *The earliest mention of Guayabo is in a record of a journey made by the Governor Carrandi Menón through the area in 1738; however, the pre-Columbian remains were only properly discovered in the late 1800s, by the explorer Anastasio Alfaro, and it was not until 1968 that systematic excavations began.*

Realizing its importance, the government made it a protected site in 1973 and the latest round of excavations began in 1987. The main problem is shortage of funds, and as the initial US grant has dwindled away, the future looks bleak. The site covers some 20ha (50 acres), of which only about one tenth has been excavated. What has emerged is a township which may have supported as many as 10,000 people, probably between the period 1000BC and AD1400, after which the site was abandoned. The reason why is not clear. It could have been an epidemic or perhaps a war with a neighbouring tribe. The excavations have revealed paved roads, houses, temple foundations and bridges. It is clear that the inhabitants were skilful in water management, having built aqueducts and water storage tanks. They were also able to bring large stones from some distance, some of which bear evidence of petrolyths, indicating a primitive form of written language. The more valuable gold and ceramic artefacts found on the site are now in the Museo Nacional in San José. The fact that the surrounding land is protected has fortunately meant that a sizeable chunk of pre-montane forest has survived on the site, which supports a varied bird population. Guayabo is open daily 08:00–16:00, National Park fee payable on entrance.

The Central Valley at a Glance

BEST TIMES TO VISIT

With its equable temperatures, the Central Valley is an all-year-round destination, but the **dry season** from December to March sees the most foreign tourists. For the remainder of the year, afternoon rain is normal and in the higher, more remote areas, a 4WD vehicle is advisable.

GETTING THERE

Most visitors to the country will arrive through **Juan Santamaría airport**, on the outskirts of Alajuela and linked to other parts of the country via domestic flights.

GETTING AROUND

The **road** network is well served by a range of private bus companies. Timetables can be obtained from ICT in San José. Car hire can be arranged at the airport or in San José, but drivers are warned that road surfaces and signposting can be poor.

WHERE TO STAY

Alajuela area
LUXURY
Xandari Plantation,
Apdo.1485-4050 Alajuela, tel: 443-2020, fax: 442-4847. Modern hotel 6km (4 miles) north of Alajuela, with pool and trails.
MID-RANGE
Hotel Alajuela,
Apdo.110-4050 Alajuela, tel: 441-1241, fax: 441-7912. Friendly town centre hotel.

BUDGET
Charly's Place, 2 blocks north of Parque Central, tel and fax: 441-0115. Small and popular with foreign backpackers.

Heredia area
LUXURY
Finca Rosa Blanca,
Apdo.41-3009 Santa Bárbara, Heredia, tel: 269-9392, fax: 269-9555. Unique country hotel with pool and restaurant.
MID-RANGE
Hotel America,
Apdo.1740-3000 Heredia, tel: 260-9292, fax: 260-9293. Modern hotel with 24 hr restaurant and roof-top views.
BUDGET
Hotel Heredia, Calle 6, Avenidas 3 and 5, tel: 238-0880, fax: 237-6622. Clean hotel in a quiet area.

WHERE TO EAT

Most of the best restaurants in the Central Valley are in the larger hotels, but there are some in rural settings which are popular with *ticos*, particularly at weekends.

La Casona del Cafetal, tel: 533-3280. Family-owned restaurant in the Orosí Valley, with views of Lake Cachí.
Banco de los Mariscos, tel: 269-9090. Outstanding seafood restaurant in Santa Barbara de Heredia.
Solar, tel: 269-6422. Costa Rican food in an old converted coffee-processing plant in San Joaquín, west of Heredia.

Green Parrot, tel: 487-7846. US-style diner in the village of La Garita. Excellent steaks.
El Mirador de Orosí, tel: 258-2422. German-owned beer garden type restaurant with international food. Next to the Orosí viewpoint.

SHOPPING

Few visitors will leave Costa Rica without paying a visit to the craft village of **Sarchí**, the country's main artisan centre, specializing in decorated ox carts. Good quality coffee beans can be bought in bulk at the end of a tour at the **Café Britt Finca**.

TOURS AND EXCURSIONS

Central Valley tours are usually arranged by tour operators based in San José, few towns in the Valley having tourist information offices.

USEFUL CONTACTS

ICT Plaza de la Cultura, Avda. Central, Calles 3/5, San José, tel: 222-1090. It can supply details of the main tourist sights in the Central Valley together with bus timetables.
SPN, Avdas. 8/10, Calle 25, San José, tel: 257-0922. The National Parks Office can give details of the reserves such as Poás and Tapantí, and organize advanced bookings.
Cartago Municipal Information Office, Avda. 2, Calles 1/3, Cartago, tel: 223-1733.

4
The Caribbean Coast

The Caribbean coastal lowlands of Costa Rica are part of the coastline which stretches from Guatemala to Panama. The lowlands are entirely within **Limón Province** and have for centuries been the most isolated part of Costa Rica, cut off by the physical barriers of the Cordillera Central and the Cordillera de Talamanca. Despite the building of the 'Jungle Railway' at the end of the last century, it was not until the **Guápiles Highway** was completed in the late 1980s that communications in the region improved.

This is the most **culturally diverse** area of Costa Rica. When Minor Keith built the railway from San José, he brought in black labourers from Jamaica and many of these people stayed on to work in the **banana plantations**. Today, around one third of the province's population of 250,000 are of **Afro-Caribbean** origin, with their own culture, Creole cooking, English patois and Protestant religion. The southern region of Limón province also has significant numbers of *indigenas*, mainly of the Bribrí and Cabécar groups.

A **tourist industry** is slowly developing along the Caribbean coast. Foreign travellers on a budget are attracted to the south of the area, particularly around Cahuita, where it is claimed there is a 'surf and drug' culture. Naturalists, particularly birders, come to the rain forests of the **Tortuguero National Park**, which also has turtle nesting beaches. Close to the Nicaraguan border, the **Barra del Colorado National Wildlife Refuge** is Costa Rica's best venue for sportfishing.

DON'T MISS

*** Tortuguero National Park: channels through the rain forest, rich in wildlife.
** Turtle Watching: four varieties of sea turtle come ashore to lay their eggs on Tortuguero's beaches.
* Barra del Colorado National Wildlife Refuge: country's main sportfishing venue.
* Cahuita National Park: observe the coral reef by snorkelling or by glass-bottomed boat.

Opposite: *Swaying palms line the golden sands of a beach near Puerto Viejo.*

CLIMATE

The Caribbean lowlands have a **hot** and **wet** tropical climate throughout the year, with average temperatures of 26°C (79°F) and between 4000mm and 5000mm (160in and 200in) of rain. There are short **dry periods**, usually in Feb/Mar and Sept/Oct but even then, **heavy showers** can be expected. **Humidity** is high.

Opposite: *The October Carnival at Puerto Limón is Costa Rica's greatest festive occasion and is claimed to rival that in Río for its vibrancy and colour.*

CARIBBEAN LOWLANDS

The old road from San José to Puerto Limón, Highway 10, follows a narrow winding route via Turrialba to Siquirres. This is rarely used now since the Guápiles Highway was opened in 1987, cutting an hour and a half off the journey. Highway 10 climbs slowly out of the Central Valley and through the Cordillera Central via the Braulio Carrillo National Park, where hill mist usually reduces visibility, before dropping down to the Caribbean Lowlands.

The first town of any note is **Guápiles**, approximately 60km (37 miles) east of San José, a largely agricultural centre which detains few tourists. Some 12km (7.5 miles) east is **Guácimo**, with an established agricultural college and a nearby flower and house plant farm, reputed to be the biggest in the world. Heading east a further 25km (15 miles) is the town of **Siquirres**, where most tourist coaches turn off through the banana plantations to the hamlet of Puerto Hamburgo to catch *lanchas* (shallow-bottomed boats) bound for the Tortuguero National Park.

Siquirres used to be an important junction on the Jungle Line. Before 1949 black operatives would be replaced here by whites for the remainder of the journey to the capital, San José. Although the Jungle Line is no longer in operation, this eastern part of the track is still used to take bananas from the inland plantations to the coast. From here it is a further 57km (36 miles) along a flat straight road to the historical carnival town of Puerto Limón.

PUERTO LIMÓN

The capital of Limón province, Puerto Limón and its suburbs contain around 70,000 people. It is a busy port, but has lost much of its trade in recent years to **Moín**, some 8km (5 miles) to the northwest, where the larger banana boats make use of the deeper water. Offshore is the small and rocky island of La Uvita, where Columbus made his first landfall on what is now Costa Rica. Because of earthquake destruction Limón today sadly has none of the rather delapidated architectural charm

of some other Central American ports. The town has a generally run-down look about it, though there are a few reasonable hotels and a beach resort at **Playa Bonita**.

In the centre of Puerto Limón is **Vargas Park**, with a bandstand, shady royal palms with a family of sloths and some faded murals showing the history of the port. A bronze bust of Christopher Columbus and his son Fernando, which was erected in 1990 as part of the 500th anniversary of the landing, looks out over the Caribbean. Apart from the **Town Hall**, with some interesting iron grillwork, there is little else to see. Visitors staying longer should be very aware of street crime, particularly after dark.

The main reason for going to Puerto Limón is the annual **Carnival**, which takes place in the week of 12 October (Columbus Day). It is very popular with *ticos* and hotels are always fully booked. Don't try to swim in the sea here – the municipal pool has closed and the sea is badly polluted by the banana boats.

CARNIVAL IN LIMÓN

The annual Carnival in Limón is held for a week around Columbus Day (12 October) and attracts Costa Ricans from all over the country. Hotels are fully booked for weeks ahead for the *ticos'* biggest festival of the year. The highlight is the street parade, with outrageous costumes, ornate floats and deafening music, while discos, dancing, bull running, reggae, street theatre and fireworks add to the atmosphere. Although vast amounts of alcohol are consumed, there is an alcohol-free zone especially for children and families.

Things improve to the south of Puerto Limón, where Highway 36 runs to the Panama border at Sixaola, passing through **Cahuita**, where a marine National Park protects the coral reef, **Puerto Viejo**, one of the best surfing spots in Costa Rica, some *indigenas* reserves and the little visited but beautiful **Gandoca-Manzanillo** refuge.

THE CORAL REEF

Isla del Coco, 500km (312 miles) out in the Pacific to the southwest of mainland Costa Rica, boasts some of the best **coral reef** in the world. On Costa Rica's mainland there are only two areas of coral reef, both on the Caribbean coast. The main reef is just off the point at **Cahuita**, the other is near the Panama border at the **Gandoca-Manzanillo Wildlife Refuge**. Coral reefs are made up of small animals called **polyps**, filter feeders which build a protective limestone layer around themselves. Over 35 types of coral have been identified at Cahuita, the most common of which are **brain coral**, **elkhorn**, **staghorn** and **fan coral**. The reefs are **under threat** due to the chemical pollution from the plantations and from topsoil run-off following logging operations. Much damage was also done during the 1991 earthquake.

Cahuita

Located on a point, some 42km (26 miles) south of Puerto Limón, Cahuita is a small village with sand and gravel streets and a population of mainly English speaking blacks, the descendants of Afro-Caribbean fishermen who settled here in the middle of the last century. Tourism has developed considerably at Cahuita in recent years and the town has become popular with young backpackers. New hotels and restaurants are gradually spreading along Playa Negra (Black Sand Beach) to the north of the village, while to the south of the village is a beach of white sand backed by rain forest. Between the two is a headland, with a coral reef offshore, making up the **Cahuita National Park**. Covering a mere 1067ha (2636 acres), the park nevertheless contains a wide variety of species, both on the land and offshore. There is a trail behind the beach which passes though forest and mangroves and is excellent for a quiet morning of bird watching and monkey spotting.

There is a second entrance to the National Park leading to **Puerto Vargas**, south of the Cahuita headland. From here it is possible to take a beach path, wandering in and out of the jungle, to the southern extremity of the park at Río Carbon. This is one of the best wildlife walks in Costa Rica, with howler and white-faced monkeys, raccoons, opossums, sloths, armadillos and porcupines

Left: *Rain forest, mangroves and offshore coral reef make up the Cahuita National Park.*
Opposite: *Many simple country restaurants on the Caribbean coast serve spicy Creole cooking.*

in abundance. Birds include a variety of herons, green kingfishers and ibises, while magnificent frigate birds are always to be seen offshore. The beach is alive with land crabs and the sea affords good snorkelling opportunities – over 120 species of tropical fish have been identified here. The vegetation is also interesting and includes the breadfruit tree, believed to have been introduced to the area by Captain Bligh in 1793. It can reach 20m (60ft) in height and its glossy green leaves are often over a metre in length. The tree gets its name from its fruit, which can be cooked to give a bread-like substance which is rich in carbohydrate. Another tree found in the area is the *cawi* or sangregao. The Miskito word gave its name to Cahuita, which translates as 'the headland of *cawi* trees'.

A few kilometres north of Cahuita is the estuary of the Río Estrella, where a small wildlife sanctuary, **Aviarios del Caribe**, is based on an island in the estuary. There are numerous birds and animals at the sanctuary and popular guided kayak tours of the estuary will turn up a wide range of wildlife, including river otters, caimans and many types of heron.

CREOLE COOKING

Visitors bored with the bland beans and rice diet of the Central Valley will enjoy the more spicy offerings of the Creole cooking of the Caribbean lowlands. Creole cuisine is typified by the use of **coconut milk**, which can transform a plate of beans and rice. **Spices**, first used in Africa, figure prominently and include coriander, cumin, peppers, chillies and cloves. **Vegetables** include ackee, the potato-like yam and breadfruit. Plantains are widely used and often fried in fritters. Sweet **desserts** and **herbal teas** complete the tasty Creole menu.

TOUCANS

Toucans, of which there are six species in Costa Rica, are identified by their disproportionately large bills – despite their size these are surprisingly light. Birds of the forest canopy, they are often seen in the Tortuguero area, where they feed on fruit, seeds, insects, lizards and small snakes. Toucans nest in holes in trees, where they lay two to four white eggs. Their calls are raucously unmusical. The two largest species are the **Chestnut-mandibled toucan** and the **Keel-billed toucan**. The smaller toucans include two species of **aracari** and two species of **toucanet**.

Puerto Viejo de Talamanca

The laid-back village of Puerto Viejo de Talamanca lies 13km (8 miles) south of Cahuita. Known simply as 'Puerto Viejo', this settlement should not be confused with Puerto Viejo de Sarapiquí, further north in the country. It has become very popular in recent years with a surfing and backpacking crowd. The main attraction is without doubt the **surf**, which is the best on the Caribbean coast and arguably the finest in Costa Rica. The famous 'Salsa Brava' wave is at its best here between December and March. The village itself consists of a few dusty roads with plenty of quaint restaurants and an increasing number of accommodation possibilities.

A local organization called **ATEC** (Asociacion Talamanqueña de Ecoturismo y Conservación), which is devoted to ecologically sustainable development, runs tours, including guided walks through local forests and to the local Bribrí **KeköLdi Reserve**. It also offers snorkelling trips to the reef and fishing trips in dugout canoes.

The road south from Puerto Viejo has recently been paved, making it easier to reach the small villages of **Punta Uva** and **Manzanillo**, with superb sandy beaches backed by coconut palms. Even further south, stretching all the way to the Panama border, is the **Gandoca-Manzanillo Wildlife Refuge**, consisting of around 65 per cent rain forest. Rarely visited, it has recorded some 350 species of birds and four types of sea turtle nesting on its beaches. There is also an offshore coral reef, which is in better shape than the one at Cahuita, offering some excellent snorkelling possibilities. The peaceful Gandoca estuary, backed by vibrant red mangroves, is said to provide a home for the endangered manatee.

Below: *Puerto Viejo is famed amongst surfers for its 'Salsa Brava' wave: the best surfing conditions are between December and March.*

Left: *The pace of life in Puerto Viejo is slow and relaxed; reggae emanates from laid-back restaurants lining the village's few rough roads.*

NORTH FROM PUERTO LIMÓN

While the area to the south of Puerto Limón is mainly visited by independent travellers, the coast to the north is the domain of package tourists, who come to visit the Tortuguero National Park for its wildlife and turtles, or go to the Barra del Colorado area for game fishing. The deepwater port of **Moín**, some 8km (5 miles) northwest of Limón, used to be the starting place for boat trips along the canal to the Tortuguero, but the 1991 earthquake raised land levels to such an extent that only the most shallow-bottomed boats can now follow this route and most of the package tour traffic uses **Hamburgo de Siquirres**. From here the *lanchas* follow the Río Reventazón through lush banana plantations and cleared cattle land to its shallow mouth and the sportfishing resort of **Parismina.** From there the boats travel northwest along the wide coastal canal, constructed so that traffic can avoid the Caribbean surf. The route passes through rain forest and past small clearings with settlements often built on stilts, while the busy boat traffic and abundant wildlife lead to justifiable descriptions of an 'Amazon African Queen experience'. This, for many visitors, will be the highlight of their holiday.

STAYING IN A JUNGLE LODGE

The main accommodation option for visitors coming to the Tortuguero area is to stay in a **jungle lodge**. There are around 10 lodges within a few miles of the village, many of them on the waterside. Some, such as **Mawamba Lodge** and **Tortuga Lodge**, have won Eco-tourism awards, but most are fairly basic wooden buildings with verandas and rooms with cold showers, fly screens and fans. Food is wholesome. Some, such as **Jungle Lodge**, have trails running into the rain forest. Most of the lodges have canoes for hire and can provide **guides**. Tours to observe the **turtle nesting** can be arranged.

TURTLE WATCHING

The most memorable
experience for a visitor to
the Tortuguero National
Park is to watch the turtles
nesting. There are five species
of marine turtle seen at
Tortuguero and four of these
breed regularly. The largest is
the **leatherback**, whose shell
or carapace can grow to 5m,
making it the largest reptile
in the world. The commonest
is the **green turtle**, which
comes ashore in huge
numbers, known as
arribadas. The **hawksbill
turtle** has a distinct hooked
'beak' and tends to nest
singly. The **olive ridley
turtle** is more commonly
seen on the Pacific coast,
while the **loggerhead**,
although often spotted along
the Caribbean shore, appears
not to nest in Costa Rica.

Tortuguero National Park ★★★

This extensive park covers some 19,000ha (46,080 acres)
of coastline and adjacent rain forest, which is under considerable threat on its landward side both from loggers
and agricultural practices. It has a hot, steamy climate
with no clear dry season and an annual rainfall of over
5000mm (200in), so that rainwear (cape and rubber
boots) is an essential item of luggage.

The rainfall of just one month, such as September, can
equal the total annual rainfall for many places on the
central plateau. Humidity is high, with 85 to 90 per cent
in the 'drier' months of the year, such as March, but
rising from 95 to 99 per cent in the wetter periods. For
visitors who arrive unprepared for such dampness, most

lodges provide
capes and boots.

The national
park's name is
derived from the
word *tortuga*, the
Spanish name
for turtle, and

four types of sea turtle nest on the beaches here at various times between February and October every year. In addition there are a number of river turtles to be found along the forest waterways.

Visitors generally stay in **jungle lodges**, most of which are located near to **Tortuguero Village** in the northeast corner of the park. Tortuguero lies on a narrow strip of land, two or three hundred metres wide, between the Caribbean Sea and Tortuguero Canal. It is a soporific village of around 600 people, with palm groves, well-mown lawns and a profusion of tropical shrubs. Sandy paths run around the settlement with its wooden houses with tin roofs, an attractive little church and the occasional store or bar. There is a small information kiosk in the centre of the village and close by is a new **Visitors Centre**, which shows a brief video on turtle conservation. There is a short, but well-maintained **nature trail** nearby. A donation on entry to the Centre is much appreciated. Open 09:00–12:00 and 14:00–17:00.

Next to the canal-side jetty is a surprisingly well-stocked souvenir shop. Just 3km (2 miles) north of the village is a small airstrip, with daily flights to San José. The **beach**, where the turtles nest to the seaward side of the village, is rather scruffy and not suitable for swimming due to the rip tides, sharks and barracudas, but there are usually sea birds such as royal terns, frigate birds and brown pelicans flying past, and waders such as plovers and sand-pipers occur along the shoreline.

A short boat ride from the village brings the visitor to the **Caño Palma Biological Station**, a Canadian-run organization, which runs guided treks through the rain forest and up to local viewpoints.

> **ANTS OF THE FOREST**
>
> There are several ant species in the rain forests, including **bullet ants**, whose bite can be fatal, and **army ants** who form a swarm of often over a million to attack their prey. The most noticeable ants, however, are the **leaf cutter ants**, often seen in long lines crossing forest trails and carrying leaf pieces to their underground colony. The leaves decay to form a mulch, which eventually develops fungus. The fungus is then fed to the ant colony.

Below: *Boat is the main form of transport in the humid rain forest of Tortuguero National Park.*
Opposite above: *Floating water hyacinths conceal a caiman at Tortuguero.*
Opposite below: *Tortuguero's waterways provide a home for a wide variety of herons and egrets.*

SHARK TERRITORY

For much of the Caribbean shore, **swimming** is not a serious option. Rip tides, heavy waves and pollution from banana boats are just some of the hazards. The main danger, however, is the presence of **sharks**. Many come into quite shallow water and are serious predators of baby turtles scuttling into the sea, while at certain times of the year, snorkelling and surfing can be hazardous. A dangerous species is the **bull shark**, which is often seen in the Barra area migrating up the Río San Juan to breed in the fresh water Lake Nicaragua. Species which are able to move from salt to fresh water without apparent ill effect are described as **euryhaline**.

The forest and waterway areas of Tortuguero abound with **wildlife**. The canals, rivers and creeks are said to have 50 types of fish, plus caimans, crocodiles, river otters and seven types of fresh water turtle. Manatees can occasionally be seen under the water. The exotic shrubs in the grounds of the lodges attract swarms of butterflies when the sun is out. Mammals include three types of monkey, jaguars, anteaters, sloths and numerous species of bat, one of which catches fish by sonar. It is the birds, however, which are most impressive and more than 400 species have been recorded in the park. Jacanas can be seen on the water hyacinth rafts, while kingfishers, herons, anhingas and egrets skulk in the waterside vegetation. Parrots, toucans and trogons are noisy in the forest trees, while humming-birds are easily attracted to the sugar water feeders in the grounds of the lodges. Canoes can be hired to explore the rivers and creeks, with early morning being the best time for the maximum number of sightings. Some smaller wildlife, however, is less welcome and visitors should come well-stocked with some form of insect repellent.

Accommodation is limited to simple, clean *cabinas* in Tortuguero village and around ten 'jungle lodges', which are heavily used by two and three-day package **tours** from San José. The two lodges on the village side of the canal have the advantage of the facilities of the village and proximity of the turtle beach. The other lodges need to transport their visitors by boat. Most tours include guided forest walks, boat trips and turtle watching if it is in season. Some tours provide a walk to the top of **Cerro Tortuguero**, an old volcanic plug in the north of the area, which rises to 119m (390ft) and gives superb views over the surrounding forest, waterways and coast.

Barra del Colorado National Wildlife Refuge *

The Barra del Colorado National Wildlife Refuge, situated between Tortuguero and the Nicaraguan border, is a remote and sparsely populated part of the country, covering some 92,000ha (227,000 acres). It is best reached by plane, a 30-minute flight from San José which operates on a daily basis. Access by road is limited: the dirt road system ends at **Puerto Lindo** on the western side of the reserve and from there travel is by boat along the Río Colorado. It is also possible to travel by boat from **Puerto Viejo de Sarapiquí**, a tranquil three-hour trip down river.

The reserve is largely comprised of the delta of the **Río San Juan**, which forms the border with Nicaragua and drains Lake Nicaragua. The Río Colorado is the main distributary on the Costa Rican side of the border and it is at the mouth of this river that one finds the village of **Barra del Colorado**, divided into Barra Norte on the river's north side and Barra Sur to the south. The airstrip is at Barra Sur.

Above: *Exotic butterflies settle readily on the various flowering shrubs around the lodges of Tortuguero National Park.*

Opposite: *Laguna Lodge is one of several lodges in the Tortuguero National Park which provide basic accommodation for tourists seeking out the wildlife of the rain forest; many of the lodges hire out canoes and provide knowledgeable guides to accompany visitors on walks in the forest.*

RIVER CRAFT

Roads are scarce along the land bordering the Caribbean coast and most local traffic is water-borne. The traditional dug-out canoe is still widely used, although outboard motors are gradually replacing the paddle. The water buses of the area are the **lanchas**, which are long, narrow boats capable of carrying up to 30 people. The canal which runs parallel to the coast from Moín to Barra del Colorado was once capable of taking large boats, thereby avoiding the treacherous waters of the Caribbean, but the 1991 earthquake raised the level of the land by 1.5m (5ft) and now only shallow draught craft can use the waterway.

Below: *Traditional dugout canoes are still seen around the waterways of Barra del Colorado, where roads are almost non-existent.*

The 2000 or so inhabitants of the river delta are a mixture of Afro-Caribbean, *indigenas*, Costa Ricans and some Nicaraguans who fled across the border during the Civil War. Barra's proximity to the instability in Nicaragua has held up tourist development, but this is certain to change in the not too distant future.

With an average temperature of 26°C (79°F) and an annual rainfall of 4000mm (160in), Barra has a similar climate and natural vegetation to Tortuguero. The wildlife is equally good, but less accessible as there are few trails and most viewing is by boat. Crocodiles, sloths, monkeys and iguanas are bound to be seen, along with a wide range of water and forest birds. This is also the best location in Costa Rica to see the endangered manatee go gliding past under the water.

Most people, however, come to Barra del Colorado for the **sportfishing**. The best season for tarpon is from February to May, while snook are caught in droves during September and October, though there is good fishing to be had at any time of the year. Other fish available include barracuda and rainbow bass, while there is deep sea fishing for both marlin and sailfish. Most lodges operate a 'catch and release' policy. Tours are arranged in San José and consist of three or five-night packages with accommodation, food, equipment and boats provided. A few of the lodges also provide certain package arrangements for naturalists wishing to study the area.

The Caribbean Coast at a Glance

With year-round heavy rainfall in the north of this region (most places record 3000–5000mm;120–200 in), visitors will get wet whatever time they visit. There are, however, slightly drier times, between February and March and September and October, and the south is much drier.

Puerto Limón can be reached from San José by the **Guápiles Highway**, which extends south to the Panama border. **Travelair** and **SANSA** operate domestic flights from San José to Barra del Colorado and Tortuguero.

Except on the main highway, **road** transport is confined to dirt roads. North of Moín, transport is almost entirely by **boat**. There are no scheduled flights between settlements.

There is nothing in the luxury range along the coast, but plenty in the budget category.

Puerto Limón
No budget stays can be recommended in Limón. Prices can be raised as much as 50% during **carnaval** week.
MID-RANGE
Hotel Acón, Avenida 3/3, apdo.528, Puerto Limón, tel: 785-1010. Clean rooms, restaurant, 2nd-floor disco.

Cahuita
MID-RANGE
Hotel Magellan, Apdo.1132, Puerto Limón, tel and fax: 755-0652. North end of Playa Negra, tidal pool, restaurant.
BUDGET
Hotel Cahuita, next to National Park, tel: 755-0233. Motel-style cabins with pool.

Puerto Viejo
MID-RANGE
Hotel Maritza, tel: 758-3844. Small beach front hotel, bar.
Shawanda, 8km (5 miles) of Puerto Viejo, tel: 750-0018, fax: 750-0037. Thatched buga-lows 200m from the beach.
BUDGET
Cabinas Jacaranda, tel: 750-0069. Cabins set in a landscaped garden.

Tortuguero
Tortuga Lodge, tel: 257-0766, fax: 257-1665. Owned by Costa Rica Expeditions. The areas most comfortable lodge.
Ilan Ilan Lodge, owned by Mitur Tours, tel: 255-2031. The most basic of the lodges.
Pachira Lodge, Costa Rican-owned, tel: 256-7080. 40 rooms. Restaurant and pool.
Mawamba Lodge, tel: 223-2421, fax: 222-4932,

Apdo.6618, 1000 San José. The most up-market lodge.

Barra del Colorado
Silver King Lodge, tel/fax: 381-1403.The most de luxe lodge. No expense spared.

Puerto Limón
Springfields, tel: 758-1203. Best Creole food in town.

Cahuita
Miss Edith's, north end of the village. Renowned throughout the region for its fish stew.

Puerto Viejo
Garden Restaurant, near the football field. Superb Trinidadian food.
Tamara, in the heart of town. Caribbean cooking with good seafood. Clean and laid back.

Tortuguero
Miss Junie's, north end of the village. A legend in the area. Jerk chicken a speciality.

ATEC (Talamanca Association of Eco-tourism and Conservation), tel and fax: 798-4244. Puerto Viejo's private information bureau.

PUERTO LIMÓN	J	F	M	A	M	J	J	A	S	O	N	D
AVERAGE TEMP. °F	77	78	79	80	80	80	79	80	81	79	78	78
AVERAGE TEMP. °C	25	25.5	26	26.5	26.5	26	26	26.5	27	26	25.5	25.5
RAINFALL in	12.8	7.5	7.7	11.8	11.4	9.5	15.8	1.2	4.9	7.5	13.8	19.3
RAINFALL mm	32.5	190	195	300	290	240	400	250	125	190	350	490

5
The Northern Zone

The northern zone of Costa Rica, the Zona Norte, stretches from the **Cordillera Central** to the border with Nicaragua. Despite the zone's proximity to Nicaragua it was unaffected by the hurricane which recently battered that country. The mountain area is dominated by the active cone of **Volcán Arenal**, rising to 1633m (5358ft). Further north, stretching towards the border, and to the west, are the tropical plains known as *llanuras*. The northern boundary with Nicaragua is marked by the **Río San Juan**, the border officially on the Costa Rican bank.

The **climate** is hot and wet, though with a distinct dry season in the northwest. Parts of the *llanuras* are flooded during the wet season, resulting in an excellent habitat for migrating wildfowl. The vegetation of the region is mainly scattered forest and grassland, with the trees packed more densely towards the east. Much of the woodland, however, has been cleared for cattle *fincas*, banana plantations, rice and fruit growing.

The northern lowlands have a small and scattered population, a poorly developed infrastructure, largely inadequate roads badly served by public transport and a poor choice of accommodation for the visitor. Access to the area by air is now much improved with both SANSA and Travelair offering flights between San José and Fortuna. Tourist potential, however, is good. The small town of **Fortuna** is developing as a centre from where tourists can fan out to **Arenal Volcano**, and to the huge but under-visited **Caño Negro Wildlife Refuge**. In contrast there is the **Monteverde Cloud Forest Reserve**,

DON'T MISS

*** Monteverde Cloud Forest: Costa Rica's most popular reserve, with forest trails, epiphytes and quetzals.
** Arenal Volcano: the country's most active volcano.
** Tabacón Hot Springs: volcano-watch while soaking in a hot stream.
** Caño Negro Wildlife Refuge: wetland reserve with abundant birds and reptiles.
* Lake Arenal: windsurfing, sailing and angling on Costa Rica's largest lake.

Opposite: *Tourists explore Monteverde Cloud Forest Reserve, one of the most popular in Costa Rica.*

CLIMATE

The area is **hot** and **wet** all year, though in the west, near Guanacaste province, there is a **drier season** from January to March. The mountains in the south of the area are chilly and often **cloud covered**. Humidity is high.

Below: *The slow-moving sloth is found in forests and parks all over Costa Rica.*

which at times has more visitors than it can cope with. Another town which is developing its tourist potential is **Puerto Viejo de Sarapiquí**, where there are a number of eco-lodges such as **Rara Avis** and **Selva Verde**.

PUERTO VIEJO AND AROUND

A town of around 6000 inhabitants, Puerto Viejo de Sarapiquí is 100km (62 miles) northeast of San José. It can be reached by one of two routes. The eastern route follows Highway 32 through the Braulio Carrillo National Park and down the Pacific slope until, just short of Guápiles, Highway 4 is followed northwards directly to Puerto Viejo. There are no towns of importance on the way, but the road surface is good and this is the route most likely to be followed by the tour operators' coaches.

The western option is far more scenic, peaceful and interesting, but much slower. It follows Highway 126 north from San José, using a pass through the Cordillera Central, with Volcán Barva on one side and Volcán Poás on the other. This leads to a truly spectacular descent to the northern lowlands, passing a number of pristine waterfalls and following the Río Sarapiquí all the way to the small market town of Puerto Viejo.

There is little of interest in Puerto Viejo itself. It was once an important river port, sending goods down the Sarapiquí to the Río San Juan and on to the sea. Other modern forms of communication have now superseded this function, but keen tourists can still hire motorized dugouts for river trips. Otherwise, the town seems to operate mainly as a local market centre for the surrounding fruit plantations. Puerto Viejo does, nevertheless, make a good jumping off point for visits to nearby eco-lodges and biological research stations.

La Selva Biological Research Station *

Located a mere 4km (2.5 miles) south of Puerto Viejo, La Selva is owned by the Organization of Tropical Studies and concentrates on research into the biological aspects of rain forests and other tropical habitats. Although research is the main focus of the station, visitors are welcome and there are some 25 trails through primary and secondary forest, abandoned farmland and pasture land. Not surprisingly, there is abundant wildlife to see, with over 400 species of birds recorded and 120 types of mammals as well as a host of insects and plants. With over 4000mm (160in) of rain falling annually, expect the trails to be muddy.

Rara Avis *

Situated 18km (11 miles) south of Puerto Viejo, RaraAvis is a private rain forest reserve, founded by **Amos Bien**, a North American biologist who came to Costa Rica as a student and never went home. The reserve covers approximately 1330ha (3280 acres) of pristine land and is approached directly from Highway 4 at Las Horquetas, from where there is a bone- jarring two-hour tractor journey to the wel- coming lodge.

> ### SLOTHS
>
> One of the oddest mammals in Costa Rica is the sloth, found countrywide. There are two types, the **brown-throated three-toed sloth**, which is active by day, and **Hoffman's two-toed sloth**, which is largely nocturnal. Sloths have a low metabolism and move extremely slowly. They are difficult to spot in trees, partly because their fur is often covered with algae. Sloths descend from their arboreal territory once a week to defecate. The defecations fertilize the tree, which is then left to the sloth's single baby when it matures, the adult moving on to find another home.

Below: *Many mature rain forest trees are typified by immense buttress roots.*

Above: *The drier north-western regions of Costa Rica specialize in cattle ranching; the most common breed of cattle here is the floppy-eared Brahmin, which can withstand the dry conditions.*

Opposite: *Agriculture is also an important industry in the area around San Carlos; roadside stalls sell a wide variety of fruit and vegetables.*

THE JESUS CHRIST LIZARD

One of the strangest and most attractive amphibians in Costa Rica is the Jesus Christ lizard or **basilisk**. This bright green lizard is usually seen along forested river banks. The males have a long crest running along the length of their body and elongated webbed hind feet which allow them to literally 'walk on water' when they are suddenly disturbed.

Rara Avis concentrates on showing that the rain forest can be both profitable and sustainable without being destroyed. A wide variety of the forest specimens have been developed as ornamental house plants, raw material is used for wicker work and small family-run butterfly farms have been set up. Rara Avis is also the place where canopy platforms and cabins were first developed, and where Donald Perry developed his prototype of the aerial tram.

Rara Avis can be visited on package tours from San José, with two standards of accommodation offered. The cheaper option is at El Plástico, the site of a former convicts' colony, while the more up-market Waterfall Lodge offers comparative luxury. Over 350 species of birds have been recorded at Rara Avis, plus a good variety of mammals including three types of monkeys. Around 500 species of trees have been recorded, while snakes include the deadly fer-de-lance and bushmaster.

Selva Verde *

Located 7km (4.3 miles) west of Puerto Viejo, on the side of the Río Sarapiquí, Selva Verde is owned by an American travel firm and is purely a tourist lodge, carrying out no research. Covering some 200ha (494 acres) of forest, swamps and pasture land, it has a variety of walking trails, a medicinal plant garden, a wild butterfly garden and a comprehensive reference library. It also offers boat trips, white-water rafting and horse riding.

SAN CARLOS

The road west of Puerto Viejo passes through a series of small market towns, such as **San Miguel** and **Aguas Zarcas**, until **Ciudad Quesada** is reached. Quesada is better known to its 30,000 inhabitants as **San Carlos** and is a busy market centre for ranching and agriculture at the boundary of the Cordillera Central and the *llanura* to the north. Its biggest event of the year is the *Feria del Ganado* or cattle fair held every year in April. San Carlos is also the main centre in Costa Rica for making saddles and there are a number of *talabarterías* or saddle shops in the town centre. Few tourists stay in San Carlos, preferring the area further west, where there are a handful of luxury resorts, such as the **El Tucano Country Club**, where hot springs lead into a number of pools with reviving thermal waters. Amongst its other attractions are Turkish baths, saunas, a fitness and jogging track, tennis and horse riding.

RAINFOREST MAMMALS

Costa Rica's forests are rich in mammals. All visitors hope to see the jaguar and other members of the cat family, but they are rarely lucky – a paw mark on a muddy trail is the best most people can hope for. There are many other mammals, however, which with luck and patience can be seen. The **armadillo**, with its 'armour plating', is unmistakable. It forages noisily in the leaf litter in pursuit of insects and, with its poor eyesight, has often been known to bump into the feet of watchers. The **racoon** is smaller than its North American cousin, favouring waterside locations but taking to the trees if disturbed. Also common is the **coati**, which spends much of its time snuffling around the forest floor, but is equally at home in trees, where it copulates and sleeps. The **agouti** looks like a cross between a rat and a rabbit and is often seen running quickly along the forest floor. There are also five species of **squirrel**.

STRICTLY FOR VULCANOLOGISTS

Although climbing to the crater of the highly active **Volcán Arenal** is forbidden (many people have broken this rule and not lived to tell the tale), keen volcano watchers have plenty to interest them in the **Fortuna** area. Popular are **night tours**, when the molten lava and rock bombs can give an impressive 'fireworks display'. These pyrotechnics can also be observed while soaking in the hot streams at **Tabacón**. The ultimate observation point is at the **Arenal Observatory Lodge**, a station set up by the Smithsonian Institute offering simple accommodation. Make time to visit the **Museum of the World's Volcanoes** just outside Fortuna on the Arenal road. Open Tuesday–Sunday 10:00–22:00.

FORTUNA AND LAKE ARENAL

Officially known as La Fortuna de San Carlos, this small town of 7000 people was once a minor agricultural settlement, but has now become a lively tourist centre, largely because it is the nearest place to the impressive cone of **Arenal Volcano** and its surrounding National Park. Other tourist locations within reach include **Lake Arenal**, with fishing and windsurfing possibilities, **La Catarata de Fortuna** waterfall, the **Tabacón Hot Springs Resort** and the **Caño Negro Wildlife Refuge**.

Fortuna itself is a friendly little town centred around a wide open space which doubles as a soccer field. The simple church with its latticework tower on the western side of the field makes a contrasting foreground to the cone of Volcán Arenal 5km (3 miles) away to the southwest. There is a tourist information office in the main street in Fortuna, while a number of tour operators (most based in hotels) can supply details of excursions.

Excursions from Fortuna
Volcán Arenal *

Rising to 1633m (5358ft), Arenal is everyone's idea of what a volcano should look like, with its perfect cone shape and frequent spectacular activity. After lying dormant for hundreds of years, the volcano erupted violently in 1968, sending ash, volcanic bombs and lava

over a wide area. The village of Tabacón was totally destroyed and over 60 of its inhabitants killed, along with thousands of cattle. Since then, it has been Costa Rica's most active volcano, erupting on an almost daily basis. Needless to say, it is extremely dangerous and foolish to walk anywhere near to the summit, with its crater some 150m (492ft) deep and the eruptive activity highly unpredictable. It is possible to hike

VULTURES

Look up into the skies of
Costa Rica. Any black speck
to be seen floating around in
the thermals is likely to be a
vulture. Vultures are most
easily identified by their
underwing pattern. The most
widespread type is the **black
vulture**, which has light grey
tips to its wings. The black
vulture is catholic in its
feeding habits and, as well
as carrion, it will eat fruit,
while it is also a predator of
baby sea turtles. The **turkey
vulture** is also common and
has a broad light grey area
along the length of the rear
part of the underwings. The
king vulture is the largest
vulture seen in Costa Rica
and other vultures will give
way to it at a carcass. It is
white in colour, but has black
on the rear part of its wings.
The **lesser yellow-headed
vulture** is rare and confined
to wetland areas, where it
will eat the bodies of reptiles
and fishes. In appearance, it
is similar to the turkey
vulture, apart from its
distinctly coloured head.

around its base, but most tours view the volcano from
the west and north sides where there are fresh lava
flows. The summit is often cloud-covered during the
day, but night viewing can be spectacular, with glowing
lava flows and red hot rocks being thrown from the
crater. **Arenal National Park** covers some 2920ha (7215
acres) around the volcano. Access within the park is
restricted, but this is not a problem as many of the best
views of the volcano are outside the park boundary.

Balneario Tabacón *

Most of the streams flowing off the flanks of Volcán
Arenal have been naturally heated and are often full of
beneficial minerals. At Balneario Tabacón, some 12km
(7.5 miles) west of Fortuna, a valley with a hot stream
has been converted into a complex of eight pools of
various temperatures ranging from 27°C (80°F) to 39°C
(102°F). The largest pool has a water slide and swim-up
bar. There are also several waterfalls, the largest of
which has a rock ledge which makes a popular place to
sit for a free shoulder massage. Mud packs and massages
are available on request.

Above: *The church at
Fortuna, a town rapidly
developing as a tourist
centre, features a distinctive lattice-work tower.*
Opposite: *The most
dangerous of Costa Rica's
eight active volcanoes is
Volcán Arenal, with its
perfect cone shape.*

Above: *Rolling hills make up the landscape between Tilarán and Monteverde.*

ECO-TOURISM

Costa Rica has been described as one of the world's great eco-tourist destinations, but there is considerable debate as to what the term means. It is generally viewed as 'responsible' tourism, whereby small-scale ventures operate in a manner which does not destroy local habitats and has sincere consideration for native cultures. The tourism should be sustainable and actually strengthen the conservation effort. Costa Rica largely satisfies this definition. Hotels are mostly small scale, while in the national parks, revenue helps fund scientific research. Tourism provides work for locals, but in such a way that they are involved in preserving their environment.

The landscaped grounds with their exotic shrubs have a trail which is floodlit at night. Many tour operators bring groups in the evening, and one of the great Costa Rican experiences is to loll in the thermal stream at Tabacón and watch Volcán Arenal erupt. Open daily 10:00–22:00. Across the road is a less expensive thermal alternative, but with fewer facilities.

La Catarata de Fortuna *
The Río Fortuna Waterfall is reached by a 4.8km (3 mile) dirt road from Fortuna. This leads to a lookout point, from where it can be seen that there are in fact two waterfalls, the upper being the most impressive, cascading in a narrow ribbon through the rocks and forest. It is another 20 minutes' muddy scramble to reach the falls themselves, where swimming is possible.

Laguna de Arenal *
Lake Arenal, situated about 18km (11 miles) west of Fortuna, is actually a large reservoir. Created by the Arenal dam stretching across the valley, it forms Costa Rica's largest lake, covering some 12,400ha (48 sq miles). The dam was built in 1973, the rising waters flooding both a village and a small town. A hydro-electric plant supplies electricity for the region and water is drawn off

to supply parts of Guanacaste province. The lake has proved popular for recreational activities, particularly sailing and windsurfing in the regular high winds. Arenal lake has been stocked with rainbow bass (*guapote*) and boats can be hired for angling.

A causeway runs over the dam and it is possible to drive around the lake, although the return via the south side is along a dirt track. The road along the north side passes through the small village of New Arenal and nearby are the **Arenal Botanical Gardens**, which contain over 1200 varieties of tropical plants and attract a variety of birds and butterflies. Open daily 09:00–17:00. South of the lake is the small town of **Tilarán**, which is developing a tourist industry based on the water sports on Lake Arenal.

Also near to Fortuna are the **Venado Caves**, close to the hill village of Venado. They were only discovered in 1945, when the owner of the land fell into the hole! They contain limestone features such as stalactites, stalagmites and flow deposits, and narrow passages which can be negotiated. Until recently the caves were a popular excursion for adventurous visitors. However, they have been temporarily closed following reports of visitors experiencing lung ailments after entering the caves.

SAIL BOARDING ON LAKE ARENAL

The western end of Lake Arenal is beginning to be discovered as one of the best spots in the world for windsurfing. Steady winds funnel into this far end of the lake at between 32 and 48 kph (20–30mph), providing perfect conditions for slalom blasting and chop-hopping. Add to this the pleasantly warm water and the stunning scenery and you have a perfect location. Hotels and equipment hire centres are proliferating along the southwest shore of the lake and many offer lessons for beginners in the quieter bays. The strongest winds occur between November and April, with peak conditions in January and February.

Left: *Scenic Lake Arenal offers possibilities for fishing, sailing and windsurfing.*

SI A PAZ

Following the cessation of hostilities in the Nicaraguan Civil War and the awarding of the Nobel Peace Prize to former President Arias, the **Yes to Peace** transnational park is planned to link up several existing nature reserves on both sides of the border. This should help avert the threat from multi-national firms interested in logging and plantation farming activity. Of longer standing is the **Parque Internacional La Amistad**, in the south of the country, which covers both sides of the border with Panama, and aims to protect both wildlife and the local *indigenas* groups.

Below: *Boat trips to the Caño Negro Wildlife Refuge depart from Los Chiles.*

CAÑO NEGRO WILDLIFE REFUGE **

A tour from Fortuna is the most convenient way of visiting the Caño Negro Wildlife Refuge and even this will involve a long trip by minibus to Los Chiles near the Nicaraguan border and then on by launch. The reserve, which covers around 10,000ha (24,700 acres), is seasonally flooded by the Río Frio, creating a huge shallow lake which evaporates during the dry season. For maximum bird numbers, visit Caño Negro in January or February, when the resident birds are joined by large numbers of migrating wildfowl. Common water birds include jabiru storks, anhingas, ibis, many types of heron, kingfishers and ospreys. Reptiles are easily seen and visitors are sure to spot caimans, crocodiles, 'Jesus Christ' lizards and iguanas. Mosquitoes, however, can be a problem. Many keen birders claim to have seen more species here than at Tortuguero and it seems certain that Caño Negro will be more heavily visited in the future.

A proposed development is the **Si a Paz** (Yes to Peace) transnational park, which would link Caño Negro with the reserves south of Lake Nicaragua, as well as eastwards across to the Barra del Colorado. This would create an enormous protected region and help to conserve large areas of wetland and rain forest.

MONTEVERDE AREA

Located approximately 30km (20 miles) southwest of Fortuna, Monteverde is in the higher reaches of the **Cordillera de Tilarán**, between the Arenal area to the northeast and the low hills of Guanacaste to the southwest. The journey from Fortuna is via Tilarán and rather tortuous. Travellers from San José usually approach Monteverde instead via

Above: *Horse riding excursions are available in the Monteverde area.*

the Interamericana Highway, from where there are three possible routes, all of which take about two hours to cover. Buses take the shortest route via Río Lagarto, but all three are scenic, rough and challenging, particularly in the wet season, when 4WD vehicles are essential. It has been suggested that the road to Monteverde should be paved, but this has always been resisted by the local inhabitants, who see the increased number of visitors that would result as a threat to the already fragile environment of the area.

Although synonymous with the famous **Cloud Forest Reserve**, Monteverde is actually quite a complex area. All routes pass through the village of **Santa Elena**, to the north of which is the **Santa Elena Cloud Forest Reserve**, much less visited than Monteverde, but just as rewarding. To the southeast is the straggling **Quaker settlement** of Monteverde, with numerous dairy farms set back from the road. The entrance to the Cloud Forest Reserve is at the end of the road at the top of a hill.

As one of the most popular tourist destinations in Costa Rica, the Monteverde area offers a variety of **accommodation**, but the only budget possibilities are in Santa Elena. The larger (and often quite luxurious) hotels are strung out along the road between the two villages and are heavily booked by tour groups, particularly in the drier parts of the year. With the Quaker influence strong, there is little in the way of entertainment in the evenings and bars, clubs and discos are non-existent.

QUAKERS

The Society of Friends, or Quaker movement, was started in England in the 17th century by **George Fox**. After the persecution of non-conformist sects, many Quakers moved to America. One group, led by **William Penn**, founded the colony of Pennsylvania. Pacifism has always been an essential belief of the Quakers and in Alabama, in the 1950s, a number of Quakers who had been imprisoned for refusing the draft decided to move to Costa Rica. They were impressed by the country's decision to abolish the army. They settled at Monteverde and began dairy farming. Today, Monteverde appears to be in good hands.

MAGICAL CLOUD FOREST

The cloud forests at **Monteverde** and **Santa Elena** are formed by the North East Trade winds, which having blown off the Caribbean Sea, then rise over the central mountains of Costa Rica, condensing at the colder levels and forming persistent cloud. The near 100% humidity results in an all-pervading **biomass**, with vegetation at all levels. There are few surfaces not covered in mosses, lichens and **epiphytes**, such as orchids and bromeliads. To walk through the cloud forest is to experience an eerie, wet half-light, its silence broken by the occasional echoing call of birds, an experience which can only be described as magic.

The Monteverde Cloud Forest Reserve ★★★

This private reserve was set up in 1972 with the aim of protecting the watershed above the village. More land has gradually been added over the years, so that it now covers around 17,000ha (42,000 acres) and is currently operated by the **Tropical Science Centre**. The **Monteverde Conservation League** was formed in 1986 and continues to buy additional land. The League set up a worldwide appeal in 1988 known as the International Childrens' Rain Forest Project, which raised enough money to establish the **International Children's Rainforest**, covering a further 7000ha (17,300 acres).

The Monteverde Cloud Forest Reserve covers six life zones and contains a staggering amount of wildlife, including over 400 species of birds, 490 types of butterflies, over 100 species of mammals, and 120 types of reptiles and amphibians, while 2500 species of plants have been identified. It is the luxuriant vegetation with its dripping dampness which is most impressive, with moss on every surface and lianas hanging in profusion.

A bird which everyone wants to see is the quetzal, but there are equally impressive and unusual specimens such as the bare-necked umbrella bird, with its inflatable red throat, and the three-wattled bellbird, which looks as though it is carrying worms in its bill.

There is an information centre and gift shop at the entrance to the reserve, where details may be obtained about

the reserve's seven trails, which vary in length from 200m (218yd) to 4km (2.5 miles). First-time visitors wanting to see a wide range of species could well take a guided walk. Remember that the cloud forest is both wet and cool, which means that the trails can be very muddy, especially in the wetter parts of the year. Rubber boots can be hired at the reserve and at several of the hotels in the village; also take warm clothing. The reserve is open daily 07:00–16:30. Note that only 100 people are allowed into the reserve at any one time and there may be some waiting, especially during the peak hours of 08:00–10:00 in the dry season. Tickets, however, may booked one day in advance. The adjoining International Childrens' Rainforest has one small trail, with guided tours aimed at children's groups.

Above: *Few visitors will see any of the 17 poisonous species of snake, such as this beak-nosed vine snake.*
Opposite: *An aerial tour through the forest canopy is one of many attractions in the Monteverde area.*

Santa Elena Cloud Forest Reserve **

Opened in 1992, Santa Elena is another private reserve and its administrators give a percentage of its profits to local schools. It is located 5km (3 miles) north of the village of Santa Elena and covers an area of 310ha (766 acres), consisting mainly of primary rain forest. The wildlife is similar to that in Monteverde, but as the reserve receives far fewer visitors, birds and animals are more likely to be seen. There are 10km (6 miles) of trails, with two lookout points giving superb views of Volcán Arenal, providing that the clouds are not down. There is a well-organized visitor's centre at the entrance to the reserve with interpretative displays. Rubber boots can be hired. The reserve is open daily 07:00–16:00.

HOW RESISTANT ARE THE RAIN FORESTS?

One of the scandals of the 20th century is rain forest destruction. Some experts suggest that by the year 2050 there will be no rain forest left outside protected areas, and this could well be the case in Costa Rica. The main threats come from the **logging industry**, **cattle ranching** and **plantation farming**, all major export earners for third world countries. Another approach suggests that rain forests have always suffered from destruction, for example of the **slash and burn** type favoured by many primitive forest people. All environmentalists agree, however, that future development in the rain forests must be of the **sustainable** variety.

Above: *No less than 51 species of hummingbird can be found in Costa Rica; they are readily attracted to sugar feeders such as those provided at the Hummingbird Gallery at Monteverde.*

CANOPY TOURS

One way of seeing the rain forest, which will probably only appeal to the agile and adventurous, is to take a canopy tour. These can be found in several places in Costa Rica, including Monteverde, Corcovado and Rincón de la Vieja. They consist essentially of taking a rope ladder up into the forest canopy and then traversing across on pulleys to a series of suspended platforms, from where, hopefully, interesting wildlife can be observed.

Other Attractions at Monteverde

The **Hummingbird Gallery** is beside the Monteverde reserve entrance and holds exhibitions, as well as selling paintings and giving slide shows. Outside are a range of feeders which attract hummingbirds, including the violet sabrewing, Costa Rica's largest.

Just off the north side of the road in Monteverde is *La Lechería,* or the **Cheese Factory**. It was built in 1954, three years after the first Quakers arrived in the area and now supplies 14 varieties of cheese countrywide. There are no longer guided tours, but you can watch the cheese production processes through a window in the sales room. Open Monday–Saturday 07:30–12:00 and 13:00–15:30, Sunday 07:30–12:30.

Nearby is **C.A.S.E.M.,** a local women's craft co-operative selling hand-painted and embroidered T-shirts, clothing, cards and other souvenirs. Profits go to local artists and the community in general. Open Monday–Saturday 08:00–17:00, Sunday 10:00–16:00.

The **Monteverde Butterfly Farm** near Santa Elena is unlike most of the other butterfly farms in Costa Rica, in that it concentrates on research instead of the export of pupae. Visitors are given a quick lecture, and are then taken on a tour of the farm, visiting the greenhouses where the butterflies are reared and the screened garden, where a large range of butterflies can be seen on the wing. An additional and novel feature is the glass-fronted display of a leaf cutter ant colony. Open daily 09:30–16:00.

At Santa Elena is the **Serpentarium**, a local biologist's collection of snakes that will ensure that visitors pick their way carefully along the forest trails in future. Open daily 08:00–17:00

Just 3km (2 miles) north of Santa Elena is **Rancho El Trapiche**, an old sugar mill, the wheels of which are turned by teams of oxen. A restaurant serves good food – a Marimba band plays occasionally – and home-made sugar products are sold to the public. Open Tuesday–Sunday 11:00–22:00.

The Northern Zone at a Glance

BEST TIMES TO VISIT

The **dry season**, from December to March, is the most suitable time of year to visit. During the rest of the year rainfall is high, and thick cloud sits over the mountains.

GETTING THERE

There are well-surfaced **road** links from San José to Fortuna, Ciudad Quesada and Puerto Viejo. **Buses** also run from San José to San Ramón, Los Chiles and Monteverde. An **air** service operates from San José to Fortuna.

GETTING AROUND

Roads are the only way of getting around and most of the main centres are linked by **bus** services. Road surfaces deteriorate towards the north.

WHERE TO STAY

LUXURY

El Tucano Resort and Spa, 8km northeast of Ciudad Quesada, tel: 460-1822, fax: 460-1692. Thermal waters and jogging trail in woods.

Tilajari Resort Hotel, Apdo.81, Ciudad Quesada, tel: 469-9091, fax: 469-9095. Luxurious grounds overlooking the San Carlos River.

MID-RANGE

Hotel Belmar, Monteverde, tel: 645-5201, fax: 645-5135. Swiss style hotel with valley views from balconies.

Hotel Montaña de Fuego, NW of Fortuna, tel: 460-1220, fax: 460-1455. 18 rooms with

terraces facing Arenal Volcano. Garden and nature trails.

Monteverde Lodge, Apdo.6941 San José, local tel: 645-5057, fax: 645-5126. Monteverde's best hotel with transportation to the reserves.

Hotel La Central, Ciudad Quesada, next to the park, tel: 460-0766, fax: 460-0391. Clean hotel with small casino.

Hotel San Bosco, Fortuna, tel: 479-9050, fax: 479-9109. Rooms have views of Arenal volcano. Tours arranged.

BUDGET

Cabinas Charlie, Fortuna, tel: 479-9454. Clean, friendly, popular with backpackers.

Hotel El Retiro, Parque Central, Ciudad Quesada, tel: 460-0463. Clean, basic rooms, with parking.

Pensión Santa Elena, tel: 645-5051, fax: 236-4361. Friendly and family run, with kitchen and laundry services.

Hotel Finca Valverde, between Santa Elena and Monteverde, tel: 645-5157, fax: 645-5216. Tranquil rural setting, with basic cabins, restaurant and horse rental.

WHERE TO EAT

Los Heroes, Arenal, tel: 441-4193. On the shore of Lake Arenal.

Rancho La Cascada, Fortuna, tel: 479-9145. International food and good service.

Il Vagabondsa, outskirts of Fortuna. Italian pizzeria. Lively bar with rock music.

La Carreta, Tilarán, tel:

695-6654. American/Italian food in orchid-filled gardens.

El Sapo Dorado, Monteverde, tel: 645-2952. Good vegetarian meals on terrace dining room.

El Bosque, Monteverde, tel: 645-5129. For cheaper *tico* food in Monteverde.

De Lucía, Monteverde, tel: 645-5337, fax: 645-5537 . International food. The best restaurant in Monteverde.

TOURS AND EXCURSIONS

Most excursions to the northern zone can be booked in San José, but due to the distances involved and the erratic road conditions, most of the tours consist of one or more overnight stays. There are two and three-night packages to **Monteverde**. Other well-used tours go to the **Arenal** area and the **Caño Negro Wildlife Refuge**. Many local excursions can be arranged in **Fortuna**.

USEFUL CONTACTS

Servitur, Los Chiles, tel: 471-1055. Tour operator and local information centre for the Caño Negro reserve.

Cámara de Turismo de la Zona Norte (CATUZON), tel: 460-1672, Ciudad Quesada. Provides tourist information for the northern area.

SUnión Turística Autónoma de Santa Elena y Monteverde (UTASEM), Santa Elena, tel: 645-5014. Provides information on lodging and eateries, as well as solving language problems.

6
Guanacaste and the Southern Nicoya Peninsula

Costa Rica's northwesterly province of Guanacaste has characteristics which set it apart from the remainder of the country. Its boundaries are marked on the eastern side by the Cordillera de Tilarán, which drops northwards to the lower lying, but equally volcanic, **Cordillera de Guanacaste**. Also included in this chapter is the **Nicoya Peninsula**, the southern part of which comes under the administration of Puntarenas province.

The landscape of much of the province resembles the African savanna lands. Once covered with **dry tropical forest**, this has been heavily cleared for **cattle ranching**, giving rise to the description of the area as Costa Rica's 'wild west'. Mounted on their horses, local cowboys or *sabaneros* are a common sight along the roads of Guanacaste. In the northeast of the region, a line of low-lying, perfectly shaped **volcanoes**, including Santa María (1916m, 6286ft), Rincón de la Vieja (1895m, 6217ft) and Orosí (1487m, 4878ft), offer exciting hiking trails. The Pacific coastline also provides Costa Rica's most attractive **beach holidays**, with a mixture of unspoilt bays and new resorts, such as the controversial Papagayo Project.

Guanacaste is both the hottest and the driest part of the country, the **dry season** lasting longer than in other provinces. There is much to interest **wildlife** enthusiasts, with no fewer than seven national parks and many other protected areas. A number of beaches, such as those at Playa Grande and Ostional, provide the nesting grounds for **marine turtles**. **Surfing** and **sportfishing** are also well catered for along the Pacific coast.

DON'T MISS

** **National Parks and Reserves:** Santa Rosa and Cabo Blanco for dry forest; Palo Verde for wetland species; Rincón de la Vieja for volcanic activity and Barra Honda for limestone features.
** **Pacific Beaches:** ideal for water sports and fishing.
** **Turtle Nesting:** at Playa Grande, Playa Nancite and Playa Ostional.
* **Liberia:** provincial capital with a colonial atmosphere.
* **Guaitil Pottery Centre:** pre-Columbian Ceramics.

Opposite: *Tamarindo has various hotels including the luxurious Capitán Suizo.*

CLIMATE

In the rain shadow of the cordilleras, Guanacaste is the driest part of Costa Rica. The annual rainfall for the province as a whole is 1620mm (65in), but some areas, such as the Tempisque basin, may have as little as 450mm (18in). The **dry season** lasts from November to April, when the heat can be searing. Sea breezes, however, can make the coast more bearable. The **wet season** turns the countryside green and freshens the air.

THE INTERAMERICANA ROUTE

The Pan American Highway, or Interamericana as it is locally called, runs from San José to the Pacific near Puntarenas and then follows in a direct line through Guanacaste province to the Nicaraguan border. This looks a fast route on a map, but poor road surfaces and heavy traffic means that the journey can take up to six hours. Not surprisingly, both SANSA and Travelair operate profitable domestic air flights to Liberia and the coastal resorts of Tamarindo, Tambor, and Nosara.

The Interamericana enters Guanacaste province a few kilometres north of Puntarenas. Shortly, a signpost to the right points to the town of **Juntas**, a gold mining centre around the turn of the century, attracting fortune hunters from all over the world. Although mining ceased in 1930, a small, largely open-air **Gold Museum** (Ecomuseo de las Minas de Abangares) recently opened here, making an interesting diversion from the Interamericana. Open 06:00–17:00 daily.

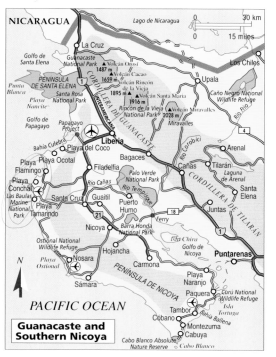

Guanacaste and Southern Nicoya

Back on the main road, there is soon a turn-off towards the west for the **Tempisque Ferry**, which saves a considerable amount of time for visitors driving to the central Nicoya resorts of Sámara and Nosara. The ferry runs every hour and the crossing takes about 20 minutes.

The next town of any size is **Cañas**, which has little of interest but makes a good base for visiting the Palo Verde National Park.

Palo Verde National Park

Created in 1982, Palo Verde consists of wetlands, dry tropical forest and low limestone hills. It is mainly of interest to birders, who will find that the dry season is the best time to visit, when the resident birds are augmented by migratory species. There is also a good chance of seeing mammals such as coati and deer on the many trails. The most attractive part of the park is the **Isla de los Pájaros** (Bird Island) in the Tempisque river, which has nesting colonies of roseate spoonbills, black crowned night herons, wood storks, white ibises and various other water birds. Tourists enjoy watching the crocodiles which usually loaf on the sand banks.

Above: *Rural buses often take the form of old American school vehicles.*
Opposite: *The important Interamericana route is heavily used by trucks.*

THE CHOROTEGAS

Of all the *indigenas* in Costa Rica, the most vibrant were the Chorotegas, the only group to have a **written language**. Excavations show that their **belief system** involved sacrifice. They were skilled artisans, working in jade, gold and pottery. Corn was the basis of their **economy** and examples exist of their carved stone *metates*, three-legged tables for grinding corn. Today many Guanacastans are happy to acknowledge their Chorotega ancestry.

INTERAMERICANA ROAD CHECKS

Police are rarely obvious in Costa Rica, but a place where their presence can be guaranteed is along the northern stretch of the Interamericana near the Nicaraguan border. Due to Costa Rica's thriving economy, jobs are often available to other Central Americans. Illegal immigrants are therefore a problem and road blocks are normal along the Interamericana. To progress speedily, make sure your passport is available and your paperwork is in order.

Below: *Fruit stores appear at frequent intervals along the Interamericana.*
Opposite: *Cowboys, or* sabaneros, *are a typical sight in Guanacaste.*

Once back on the Interamericana, the road crosses the **Río Corobicí**, well known for its fairly gentle white-water rafting. Day trips can be arranged from San José. The next town is **Bagaces**, which has little to detain the tourist and the majority of visitors hurry on to Liberia, the capital of Guanacaste province.

Liberia

Despite being a small town of barely 40,000 people, Liberia serves as the main regional and market centre of the north and an important transportation hub. It was founded by Nicaraguan settlers on the banks of the Río Liberia in the mid-18th century and for many years was known as 'Ciudad Blanca'. Of all the provincial towns in Costa Rica, it is Liberia which has the most 'colonial' feel about it. Many of the gleaming white adobe buildings are over 150 years old. Some have interior courtyards, while corner houses often have a *puerta del sol* – a door which opens in two directions in order to catch both the morning and afternoon sun. The shady **Central Park** has a rather inappropriate modern church, but an older and more interesting church, known as **La Agonia**, can be

found at the end of Avenida Central. This dates from 1852, though it looks older. The main attraction in Liberia is the **Museo del Sabanero**, which is located in the Casa de Cultura – also the local tourist information office. The Museum is well worth a visit, showing the life and history of the *sabanero* or cowboy. There are many artefacts from the old *casonas* or fortified ranches, including furniture, stoves, branding irons, saddles and ropework. The tourist information office will arrange hotel bookings and tours to national parks and working ranches.

An important date in Liberian life is 25 July, *El día de la Anexión de Guanacaste*, which celebrates Guanacaste's decision to become part of Costa Rica instead of Nicaragua. Rodeos, horse shows, fireworks and marimba bands ensure that this is a riotous occasion.

Liberia also makes a good centre for visiting the nearby coastal resorts and the string of **national parks** to the north. Liberia's **Daniel Oduber Quiros International Airport** is 12km (7.5 miles) west of the town and was built to cater for North American package tourists bound for the Nicoya beaches, thereby avoiding a transfer from the busy capital. Charter flights are now increasing. Grupotaco is the only airline that currently offers international schedule flights with a stopover in Liberia. Travelair and Lasca now offer domestic flights to Liberia.

COWBOY CULTURE

A common sight along the roads, tracks and fields of Guanacaste is the cowboy or *sabanero* who works on a cattle farm or *ganaderia*. A strong 'cowboy culture' has developed here which is every bit as evocative as that in the American 'Wild West'. *Sabaneros* are renowned as tough, hard drinking, skilled men, who live on the horse and confine their wives to the kitchen. Their skills are displayed in the local rodeos and *corridas* held throughout the Guanacaste region.

PIGS OF THE FOREST

Few forest mammals, even members of the cat family, are dangerous to walkers. An exception is the **peccary**. These animals are related to pigs and rove around in groups of up to 300. They reach 80cm (31in) and an adult can weigh up to 20kg (44lb). Peccaries can be very aggressive and noisy, clicking their teeth and grunting and even charging at people. The general advice if attacked in this way is to climb the nearest tree and wait till the peccaries get bored and leave one in peace.

Below: *Dirt roads are common and frequently become impassable in the wet season.*
Opposite: *Most of the woodland in Guanacaste is of the dry forest variety, as it has to survive through the arid season.*

NORTHERN NATIONAL PARKS

There are a number of national parks in the area north of Liberia, which together form the 110,000ha (274,000 acres) Guanacaste Conservation Area. The **Santa Rosa National Park** and the **Guanacaste National Park**, provide a 50km (31 miles) wildlife corridor, while the **Rincón de la Vieja National Park**, detached to the east, has a variety of volcanic features.

Santa Rosa National Park ★★

Santa Rosa was founded in 1971 and was the first of Costa Rica's national parks. With the addition of the Murciélago section on the northern flank, it is also one of the country's largest parks, covering nearly 50,000ha (123,500 acres). Santa Rosa has more cultural and historic interest than most other parks, as it has been the site of three battles in which invaders have been driven out of the country. The first and most famous was in 1856, when the filibuster William Walker and his men were routed at the Casona Santa Rosa, from which the park gets its name. The second battle occurred in 1919 against Nicaraguans and the third was in 1955, when the Nicaraguan dictator Somoza was put to flight. La Casona was a working *hacienda* until the park was established, but is now a visitors centre and small museum (open 07:30–16:30). All rooms are open to the public and contain exhibitions of firearms, ecology and a mock-up of a typical rustic country kitchen.

Santa Rosa, which covers most of the Santa Elena peninsula, also protects what is believed to be the largest remaining stand of **tropical dry forest** in Central America. Trails lead through the forest to a couple of excellent **surfing** beaches. One of the beaches, **Playa Nancite**, is an important nesting site for Olive Ridley sea turtles and during *arribadas* in September and October as many as 10,000 turtles can be seen on the beach.

Guanacaste National Park *

The rich wildlife corridor continues on the eastern side of the Interamericana, with the Guanacaste National Park. Opened in 1991, spurred on by the American naturalist David Janzen, it is an attempt to restore to dry forest some of the former ranchland of the area. There are few trails as yet, but with over 300 species of birds and an excellent selection of mammals, Guanacaste is sure to be a popular park to visit in the future.

Rincón de la Vieja National Park **

This national park, which covers some 14,000ha (34,600 acres), lies to the northeast of Liberia. It is named after Rincón de la Vieja volcano which rises to 1895m (6217ft), although there are other higher volcanoes in the complex. Rincón last erupted in 1991 but there is plenty of peripheral volcanic activity to see.

There are rough tracks to two ranger stations based in old *casonas*, one of which once belonged to the former US president Lyndon Johnson. From the stations it is a two day hike to the summit of Rincón and back. There is a wide variety of vegetation in the park, with high rainfall and lush forest on the Caribbean side and lower precipitation and sparser forest on the Pacific slopes. Bird life is, as usual, prolific with over 200 resident species including the quetzal and numerous parrots and toucans. The mammal list is equally impressive and includes armadillo, tapir and three species of monkeys. The park is open daily 08:00 to 16:00, the dry season being the best time to visit.

MINOR VOLCANIC ACTIVITY

Volcanoes are normally associated with explosive activity involving bombs, ash and flowing lava. Many volcanoes, however, go through **dormant** periods. During dormancy, heat remains underground giving rise to **hot springs**, which lead into rivers supporting *balnearios* or health spas. Other features include **mud springs**, *fumeroles* which are vents through which steam issues, *solfataras*, which emit sulphurous gases, and, most spectacular of all, **geysers**, where hot water is ejected to considerable height at regular intervals. These features can usually be seen in the **Rincón de la Vieja National Park**.

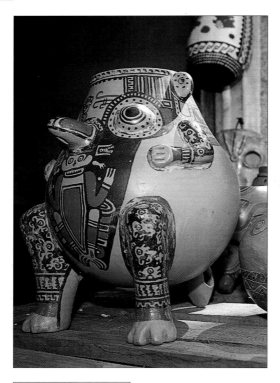

NORTHERN NICOYA PENINSULA

This peninsula runs from the Nicaraguan border for about 130km (80 miles) to Cabo Blanco in the south, bounded in the west by the Pacific Ocean and in the east by the Gulf of Nicoya and the Río Tempisque. It has long been one of the least developed parts of the country, but with the growth of tourism and the popularity of the Pacific beaches, the infrastructure is gradually improving.

From Liberia, a road leads southwest past the new airport and then heads down the spine of the peninsula, passing through the minor settlements of Comunidad, Palmira, Filadelfia and Belén, until, some 60km (37 miles) from Liberia, the ancient town of **Santa Cruz** is reached. This location is considered to be the music and folk dance capital of the country and confirms this reputation in two festivals in January and July. Much of the historic town centre was destroyed in a disastrous fire in 1991. An earthquake felled the original church in the 1950s and its ultramodern replacement with superb stained glass windows is worth viewing. Some 12km (7.5 miles) east of Santa Cruz is the ceramic centre of **Guaitil**, where the pre-Columbian pottery tradition of the Chorotega indians is healthily maintained.

A further 27km (16 miles) southeast is **Nicoya**, a town of some 25,000 people and the transportation hub of the peninsula. It is named after a Chorotega chief and many

LOCAL POTTERY

Pottery was an important Chorotega craft. Although the craft declined during the Conquest, there has been a recent revival using similar raw materials, based on archaeological research. The pottery is traditionally coloured black, red and white and decorated with animal motifs. Today, the pottery workers are mainly women and their work can be observed in the village of **Guaitil**, near Nicoya.

of the local inhabitants can trace their *indígenas* descent. The focal point of the town is the attractive Central Park and in the corner of the square is the old colonial **Church of San Blas**. Dating back to the 1600s, it contains a small museum with some pre-Columbian artefacts. Roads of varying quality feed out from Nicoya south to the Pacific resorts of Nosara and Sámara, and east to the ferry port of Naranjo. Another road leads northward to the hamlet of **Puerto Humo** on the Tempisque River, where an eco-tourist centre provides boat trips downstream to the Isla de los Pájaros section of the **Palo Verde National Park**.

Barra Honda National Park *
Mid way between Nicoya and the Tempisque River is the limestone plateau of **Cerro Barra Honda**. Although there are trails through the dry forest terrain above ground, the national park has been created to protect the underground features. The solution of the limestone has formed numerous caverns and caves filled with karstic deposits such as stalagmites and stalactites. The caves were only discovered in the 1970s, but were certainly known to the pre-Columbian indians, because their remains and artefacts have been found in the caverns, dating back to 300BC. There is also a strange array of wildlife within the caves including blind salamanders, fish and the inevitable bats. Visitors must be accompanied by a guide, who can be hired at the entrance. Visits are only allowed during the dry season, as flash floods are possible during the wetter times of the year.

LIMESTONE FEATURES

Rain is a weak acid which can dissolve limestone rocks, leaving caves and caverns underground. The lime-rich water also seeps through joints in the rock into the caves where it redeposits the lime as **dripstone** features. The best known of these are **stalactites** which form from the cave roof like icicles and **stalagmites** which build up from drips reaching the ground. These features can be seen at Barra Honda.

Left: *Santa Cruz in the north of the Nicoya Peninsula is the music and folk dance capital of Costa Rica.*
Opposite: *The Chorotega tradition of pottery has been revived at Guaitil.*

THE PAPAGAYO PROJECT

Planned to cover most of the Bay of Culebra, the Papagayo Project has aroused enormous controversy. It will include large hotels, apartments, a golf course and a marina. In all, it will provide 14,000 rooms. Environmentalists are concerned that this project is contrary to Costa Rica's eco-tourist tradition. The Mexican developers have been accused of illegally felling trees and destroying mangroves. Nevertheless it seems that Costa Rica's need for foreign investment has won out. By late 2000 the project was underway, with the infrastructure already in place. Several hotel chains, including Occidental and Four Seasons, plan to open here.

GUANACASTE COAST

The Pacific coastline of Guanacaste province and the southern Nicoya Peninsula have a string of popular beaches at intervals along the rocky coastline. There is no continuous coastal road, however, and to move from one resort to another often involves returning inland first. Many of the beaches are ideal for **surfing**, while others have become **sportfishing** centres. Some areas, such as **Sámara** and **Nosara**, have attracted wealthy North American expatriates. Beaches such as **Playa Grande** and **Playa Ostional** are nesting grounds for **marine turtles**. Traditional small-scale tourism in the area, however, is now threatened by mega-resort developments, typified by the large **Papagayo Project** in the north and the **Tambor** development in the south.

Due west of Liberia is the Bahía de Culebra. Almost the whole of this bay will be taken up with the enormous **Papagayo Project**, which within the next 15 years will provide accommodation for 28,000 people. Further south is the longer established **Playa del Coco**. Only 35km (22 miles) from Liberia and linked by a good road, it is

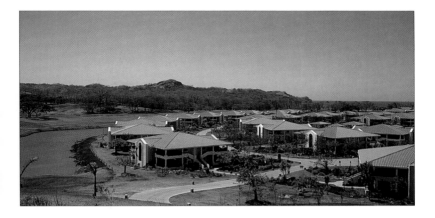

popular with young *ticos* and has a good choice of budget accommodation. It has also developed as the chief
scuba diving centre along the coast. At the southern end
of the bay is the more up-market Playa Ocotal, which
offers safe swimming and opportunities for sportfishing.

South of Ocotal is a broad headland before the next
batch of small resorts are reached. Of these, the largest is
Playa Flamingo (a name provided by developers – there
are, ironically, no flamingoes in Costa Rica). It has one of
the best white sand beaches on the Pacific coast and some
opulent villas have been constructed here. Flamingo is
renowned as the country's sportfishing capital and the
annual **International Sportfishing Tournament** is held
here during the months of May and June. Just to the
south is **Playa Conchal**, named after its pretty beach of
tiny sea shells. Conchal is the site of a massive Spanish-
owned beach and golf resort, which before the current
development of Papagayo was the largest and most
luxurious in the country.

The cape of Cabo Velas lies beyond Playa Conchal and
rounding this headland leads to the **Tamarindo** area, consisting of the long beach of Playa Grande, the Tamarindo
estuary and the resort of Tamarindo itself. **Playa Grande**
is an excellent surfing beach, but it is best known as the
nesting ground for giant leatherback turtles.

Above: *Playa Conchal
has a large Spanish-owned
resort development.*
Opposite: *Playa Grande
is one of the main nesting
grounds for marine turtles.*

PACIFIC SEABIRDS

Visitors to the Pacific beaches
cannot fail to delight in the
exotic seabirds. An elegant
black bird with a long forked
tail is the **magnificent frigatebird**. Specializing in aerial
piracy, they rob other birds of
their food. The likeable **brown
pelican** is often seen flying in
lines or diving into the waves
alongside surfers. It uses its
huge pouched bill as a sieve
to catch small fish. A graceful
white diving bird will almost
certainly be the **royal tern**.
The **brown booby** is common along the south Nicoya
Peninsula and breeds on the
islands off Cabo Blanco.

Right: *Mangroves in the Tamarindo Estuary provide a rich habitat for wildlife.*

MANGROVE SWAMPS

One of Costa Rica's most common coastal habitats is the mangrove swamp. There are five species of mangrove tree in the country and all are described as **halophytes** – plants which can tolerate salt water. They thrive on seashores, estuaries and creeks, where they can be identified by their large interlocking aerial roots. They provide a rich habitat for a range of wildlife, including roosting birds, fish and reptiles. Mangroves are often the first line of defence against coastal erosion, but are increasingly endangered because of dredging and development.

The turtles, which can reach several metres in length, are the largest reptile in the world. They come ashore to lay eggs between October and March, usually on moon-less nights. The beach, the estuary to the south, plus 22,000ha (54,000 acres) out to sea, now form the **Las Baulas Marine National Park**. Rangers strictly control the numbers of night visitors, who must be accompanied by a guide. The **Tamarindo Estuary** is flanked by mangroves and local boatmen run 'mangrove safaris', which usually turn up a variety of egrets, herons and kingfishers, plus caimans and howler monkeys.

Despite its dusty main street, **Playa Tamarindo** is one of the most popular Pacific resorts. The drive from San José takes five to six hours, but both SANSA and Travelair operate daily flights. Tamarindo offers a variety of accommodation to suit all pockets, with some hotels right on the beach, while there is a good choice of restaurants. Surfing is excellent, particularly at the river mouth, but swimmers should beware of rip tides.

The Guanacaste coast then becomes less accessible and it is not until roads lead southwest from Nicoya that resorts of any size appear. It is a 35km (22 mile) drive from Nicoya to **Playa Sámara**, which has a safe white sand beach that is excellent for swimming, as waves break in the distance on the offshore reef. Many wealthy Costa Ricans have holiday homes here and it is popular with North American package tours. Both Travelair and SANSA run daily domestic flights to Sámara.

The road from Sámara loops back northwards to the village of **Nosara**, some 5km (3 miles) inland on a low ridge. This pretty village features a riotous rodeo in January. There is a selection of nearby beaches, mostly safe for swimming and backed by luxuriant vegetation. The most northerly beach is **Playa Ostional**, which forms the main part of the **Ostional National Wildlife Refuge**, created to protect the nesting ground of the Olive Ridley turtles. The *arribadas* occur for one week at a time during the period from July to December, when the turtles arrive in their thousands, usually on dark nights just before a new moon. Locals are allowed to harvest the eggs from the first layings (which are usually destroyed by later layings); thereafter they act as guides and make sure that the remaining eggs are protected. There are only nine beaches worldwide where the Olive Ridley turtle nests and Ostional is the most important.

CROCODILES

The **American crocodile** can often be seen on the sand banks of Costa Rica's rivers. They can grow up to 5m (16ft) in length and are reputed to live for up to 80 years. These fearsome predators lay their eggs in sand banks, but probably less than 2% survive to maturity. The eggs are often trampled by cattle, while hatchlings make a tasty bite for many birds and mammals. Adults are often shot for their skins, but their biggest threat is from chemicals and other forms of **river pollutants**. The crocodile's harmless smaller cousin, the **caiman**, grows to about 1m (3ft) in length and spends much of its time in aquatic vegetation.

Below: *Surfing is excellent at Tamarindo beach, despite the presence of rip tides.*

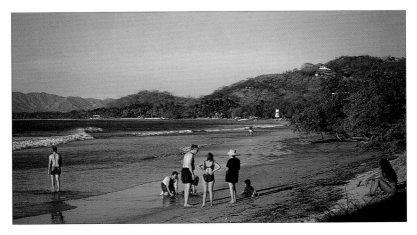

SOUTHERN NICOYA PENINSULA

The southern part of Nicoya is remote from the rest of the peninsula, largely because of the poor state of the road system. It comes under the administration of Puntarenas province and most visitors arrive in the area by ferry from the port of Puntarenas or by air from the capital San José to the new resort of Tambor.

There is a choice of **ferry**. Foot and car ferries run to the small village of **Playa Naranjo**, but as the roads inland from here are so poor, the alternative car ferry to **Paquera** is much more popular. A shuttle passenger ferry now runs directly to **Montezuma**. Car drivers should be aware that the majority of the roads in the south of the peninsula are poorly surfaced and badly sign-posted, and gas stations are few and far between.

The village of **Paquera** is 4km (2.5 miles) inland from the ferry terminal. It is a well-tended place with numerous fruit stalls along the roadside and the only gas station in the area. A short 4km (2.5 miles) south of Paquera is the privately owned **Curú National Wildlife Refuge**. Based on a working hacienda, this small reserve of 84ha (207 acres) has a variety of habitats, including primary forest, mangroves and white sand beaches where turtles nest. It has a wide range of birds and mammals for such a tiny area. To visit the reserve, call the owners on 661-2392, giving several days notice. Nearby is the beautiful uninhabited **Isla Tortuga**, a popular day trip destination from San José and Puntarenas. The island has sandy beaches backed by palm trees and other lush vegetation. Swimming and snorkelling are excellent, but avoid the weekends when it can become very crowded.

FRIGATEBIRDS

One of the more spectacular of Costa Rica's seabirds is the **magnificent frigatebird**. This elegant black bird, with its long forked tail, is commonly seen along both coastlines, acrobatically chasing and harassing other seabirds and forcing them to disgorge their latest meals. It never lands on the water, but will pluck fish and small hatchling turtles from the surface. It also concentrates around fishing boats and fish docks, where it feeds on offal. In the breeding season, the males develop a bright red pouch, which is inflated during display.

Further southwest is the small fishing village of **Tambor** on Bahía Ballena (Whale Bay). The village is in danger of being swamped by the controversial **Playa Tambor** development, currently providing more rooms than any other resort development in the country. Barceló Hotels, the sole developer of the site have built a large area of villas and a nine-hole golf course. Tambor has its own airstrip, with daily flights by SANSA and Travelair to San José.

Southwest from Tambor the road deteriorates, eventually reaching the tidy little regional centre of **Cóbano**. A road forks left here, dropping through precipitous bends to the coastal village of **Montezuma**. This settlement's dirt roads are fronted by a sandy beach, backed by palms and other luxuriant vegetation, with waterfalls plunging down from the hills behind. The surfing is good, although the swimming is affected by rip tides. The shore becomes very rocky to the southwest, with tidal pools full of colourful fish. Undeniably beautiful, Montezuma was discovered by a young, hippie set in the 1980s and has remained a popular backpackers' resort, with plenty of budget accom- modation. Local residents periodically attempt to clean the place up, but campers still line the beach taking all the shadiest spots and the noise of music resounds until the early hours. Visitors cannot be neutral about Montezuma – you either love it or hate it!

TAMBOR – A GLIMPSE OF THE FUTURE?

Tambor, the biggest resort development in Costa Rica (although it will eventually be surpassed by the Papagayo Project), has been dogged by controversy from the start. The Spanish developers have been accused of breaching several environmental laws, including destroying mangroves, taking beach sand and river gravel, building on the first 50m of beach (which should be public property) and ignoring health and safety regulations. Despite court orders and public outcry, the project has gone ahead and the developers have schemes for another eight ventures.

Below: *Montezuma and its fine sandy beach remain popular with backpackers.* **Opposite:** *A pool beneath the falls at Montezuma provides a swimming spot.*

THE FATHER OF THE NATIONAL PARKS SYSTEM

The Cabo Blanco reserve was created in October 1963 by **Olaf Wessberg**, a Swede, and his Danish wife **Karen Morgenson**, after making a worldwide appeal for funds to buy the land. It is, in fact, the oldest piece of protected land in Costa Rica and was donated to the nation long before a National Park system came into existence. Wessburg, who has been described as the 'father of the National Park system', took on many environmental causes, but was murdered in the Osa Peninsula (reportedly by logging interests) while looking at the possibility of establishing another National Park there.

Below: *The blue morpho butterfly is common in the Cabo Blanco Reserve.*

There are a number of places to visit from Montezuma. Locally, there is an attractive nature trail which runs from the northern end of the beach. It was set up by the late Karen Morgenson and it drops in and out of coves before ending up at the safe, and usually deserted, swimming beach of **Playa Grande**. At the other end of the village, a path leads to two **waterfalls**. The first is nothing spectacular, but a further 15 minutes walk up the river bed leads to an impressive cascade with a large plunge pool beneath it which is ideal for swimming and popular with the locals.

For excursions further afield, try the local tourist office in the centre of the village. Local boatmen can take visitors to **Isla Tortuga** for a fraction of the cost of the trips from Puntarenas, and scuba diving trips can be arranged. The most popular excursion is to the **Reserva Natural Absoluta Cabo Blanco**, a nature reserve some 9km (5.6 miles) southwest of Montezuma. Cabo Blanco occupies the whole of the southwest tip of the peninsula and consists of Pacific lowland tropical forest. It is named after the island offshore, where pelicans, brown boobies and frigatebirds nest, leaving a white coating on the rocks. Transport can usually be arranged from Montezuma to the ranger station. From here, a demanding trail leads for 4.5km (3 miles) to the tip of the peninsula, where there is a lovely swimming beach. The reserve is habitat to a wide range of birds and butterflies (the huge blue morpho is common), while mammals include howler monkeys, white tailed deer, squirrels, sloths and agoutis.

Guanacaste and Southern Nicoya at a Glance

BEST TIMES TO VISIT

The relatively low rainfall of the wet season means that Guanacaste is more of an all-year-round destination than other parts of Costa Rica.

GETTING THERE

Car trips from San José can be shortened by using the **ferry** across the Río Tempisque or those from Puntarenas. Visitors may choose to go by **air** from San José to Tambor, Sámara, Tamarindo or Nosara.

GETTING AROUND

Away from the Interamericana, 4WD vehicles are essential, especially in the wet. There is a reasonable **bus** network.

WHERE TO STAY

LUXURY
El Ocotal Beach Resort, Playa Ocotal, tel: 670-0321, fax: 670-0083. Jacuzzi, boats for diving and for charter.
Melia Playa Conchal, Playa Conchal, tel: 654-4123, fax: 654-4181. Beachside resort with pool, tennis, golf.
Capitán Suizo, Playa Tamarindo, tel: 653-0075, fax: 653-0292. Beachfront hotel with horses and kayaks.
Hotel Tango Mar, Playa Tambor, tel: 683-0001, fax: 683-0003. Luxury resort with reserve and golf course.
Villas Carla Luna, Tamarindo, tel: 653-0214, fax: 653-0213. Deluxe hotel and garden villas with trails to beach, pool and international restaurant.

MID-RANGE
Hotel Sugar Beach, Playa Pan de Azúcar, tel: 654-4242, fax: 654-4239. Private beach, open-air restaurant with views.
Hotel Tamarindo Diría, Playa Tamarindo, tel: 289-8616, fax: 289-8727. Beachfront hotel.
Hotel Villa Flores, Playa del Coco, tel and fax: 670-0269. Spanish colonial style hotel.
Amor de Mar, Montezuma, tel and fax: 642-0262. Wooden hotel overlooking the sea.
Hotel los Mangos, Montezuma, tel: 642-0076, fax: 642-0025. Bungalows, pool and Italian restaurant.
BUDGET
Hotel Guanacaste, nr. bus station, Liberia, tel: 666-0085, fax: 666-2287. Popular IYHF-affiliated budget hotel.
Villa del Sol, Playa del Coco, tel and fax: 670-0085. Family-style bed and breakfast.
Cabinas Zullymar, at the village loop, Playa Tamarindo, tel: 226-4732. Beach cabins.

WHERE TO EAT

El Sano Banano, village centre, Montezuma, tel: 642-0068. Health food.
San Francisco Treats, Playa del Coco, tel: 670-0484. Open air Californian café.

Stellas, Playa Tamarindo, tel: 653-0127. Italian cuisine with imaginative fish dishes.
El Ancla de Oro, Cabuya, just before the Cabo Blanco reserve, tel: 642-0023. Enjoy lobster in a rustic setting.

TOURS AND EXCURSIONS

Papagayo Excursions, Tamarindo, tel: 653-0254. Long established operator, arranging water adventures, horse rental and more.
Monte Aventuras, Montezuma, tel: 642-0025. Arranges any tour in the area.
Frontera Tours, Playa del Coco, tel: 670-0403. Arranges fishing tours, nature trips and sportfishing.

USEFUL CONTACTS

Liberia Chamber of Commerce Tourist Infor-mation Centre, Casa de Cultura, Liberia, tel: 666-1606. For internal flights contact:
SANSA, Calle 24, Paseo Colón, San José, tel: 221-9414.
Travelair, Tobías Bolaños Airport, tel: 232-7883.
For National Park reservations:
Servicio de Parques Nacionales (SPN), Calle 25, Avenidas 8-10, San José, tel: 257-0922.

LIBERIA	J	F	M	A	M	J	J	A	S	O	N	D
AVERAGE TEMP. °F	88	86	90	93	90	86	84	84	82	84	86	86
AVERAGE TEMP. °C	31	30	32	34	32	30	29	29	28	29	30	30
RAINFALL in	0.2	0.2	0.2	0.2	0.8	3.5	1.2	1.2	4.3	2.8	0.4	0.4
RAINFALL mm	5	5	5	5	20	90	30	30	110	70	10	10

7
The Southern Pacific Coast

This region stretches from **Puntarenas** in the north to the border with **Panama** in the south, a distance of nearly 300km (185 miles), and contains considerable contrasts of scenery, climate, vegetation and population. Almost the whole of the region comes under the administration of Puntarenas province.

The lowlands of the Pacific coast are backed by mountains which become less volcanic southwards. The **Fila de Bustamente** is succeeded by the lofty **Cordillera Talamanca**, rising to **Mt Chirripó**, which at 3820m (12,533ft) is Costa Rica's highest mountain. There is a pronounced dry season in the north, but further south it becomes wetter and more stiflingly humid throughout the year, with rainfall reaching in places a staggering 7000mm (275in). The natural vegetation is dry forest in the north, humid forest in the centre and rain forest in the south, but many areas have been cleared for **agriculture**, with bananas and oil palms dominating. There are numerous **national parks** and other protected areas, including the heavily visited Manuel Antonio and the remote Corcovado.

In the north is the once prosperous port of **Puntarenas**. *Josefinos* swarm to **Jacó**, their nearest resort, but those willing to travel further can find beaches ideal for surfing and diving. There are few settlements of any size in the south, where **communications** are difficult. Inland, the Interamericana runs from San José over the cloud-shrouded Cerro de la Muerte pass and on through the Valle de El General to the Panamanian border.

DON'T MISS

*** **Manuel Antonio National Park:** Costa Rica's most visited National Park, with humid tropical forest, beaches and wildlife.
** **Corcovado National Park:** wilderness experience, ideal for forest trekking and spotting endangered species.
** **Mount Chirripó:** popular hiking route to the top of Costa Rica's highest mountain.
* **Pavones:** world-famous surfing location.
* **Isla de Caño:** one of the country's best snorkelling and diving locations.

Opposite: *Lovely beaches are backed by humid rain forest in Manuel Antonio National Park.*

PUNTARENAS

Most heavy transport from San José to Puntarenas uses the Interamericana via **Palmares** and **Esparza**, but Highway 3 to the south passing through **Atenas** and **Orotina** is a much more scenic and pleasant route. South of Orotina, routes branch north to Puntarenas and south to Jacó and Manuel Antonio.

It is difficult to believe that **Puntarenas** was once Costa Rica's most prosperous port. In the 1800s, convoys of ox carts would bring coffee beans here for export via Cape Horn to Europe – a long and hazardous route. The building of the 'jungle train' to the Caribbean port of Limón sounded the death knell for Puntarenas. The recent wave of development to the south of the deep water port of **Caldera**, which can take container vessels and cruise liners, has been a further blow. Today, Puntarenas has that faded, neglected look of many tropical ports, but it remains an administrative centre and fishing port, while ferry boats ply the routes to the southern part of the Nicoya Peninsula.

The name Puntarenas means 'sandy point' and the town is built on a narrow sandy spit. A mere five avenues run east-west along the spit, while more than 50 short streets link the mangrove estuary to the north with the Pacific Ocean to the south. The estuary is almost always bustling with boats and motor yachts, many on their way to or from outings to Tortuga Island. The rather decrepit **ferry terminals** and the thriving fish dock are on the photogenic estuary side, with its mud flats, rusting hulks and lurking pelicans and frigatebirds. The Pacific shore, once the site of the thriving coffee docks, is today being redeveloped as a holiday beach. There are ambitious plans for shops, restaurants and discos on the pier of the old dock. There is little of interest in the town, apart from the **Casa de la Cultura**, which is located in an old jail and has a small museum and a pretty fountain. There is an excellent municipal **swimming pool** at the end of the point, making a welcome diversion while waiting for the ferry. It is also pleasant to sit and watch the sun sink behind the Nicoya Peninsula

SOUTH FROM PUNTARENAS

Highway 27 runs south to the modern port of **Caldera**. On the opposite side of the road is one of Costa Rica's first beach resorts, **Mata de Limón**. Located on a muddy estuary backed by mangroves, its sleepy atmosphere will soon be shattered when a new country club gets underway. From here the road heads inland towards **Orotina** and many visitors may wish to make a diversion to visit **Iguana Park**, just east of the town. This non-profit making organization breeds green iguanas and returns them to the wild. The park also has an exciting canopy tour, involving traverses from one platform to another using pulleys.

The road then heads south again to the **Río Tárcoles**. The bridge over the river is one of the best spots in the country for watching crocodiles, which are usually resting on the muddy banks, accompanied by scores of hopeful vultures.

CLIMATE

The weather varies from north to south. Puntarenas has a clearly pronounced **dry season**, when temperatures can average 30°C (86°F). Further south, the rainfall and humidity increase, with the dry season becoming progressively shorter, until, in the Osa Peninsula, **rain** falls all year round and totals can exceed 5000mm (200in). Inland, on Mount Chirripó, night temperatures may drop below freezing point.

Below: *South from Puntarenas, oil palms begin to dominate near Parrita.*

IGUANAS

There are a number of species of iguana in Costa Rica, one of which, the **green iguana**, is now endangered because of forest clearance and the fact that its meat is tasty. At **Iguana Park**, near Orotina, iguanas are bred in captivity and over 100,000 have been released into the wild. To finance this project, a certain number are sold for their meat, which apparently tastes like a 'fishy chicken'. It has been proven that iguanas can be 10 times more productive per hectare than cattle. Iguanas, which can reach 2m (6ft) in length, have learned to scavenge around human habitation and can often be seen in the grounds of hotels.

Immediately south of the bridge is the **Carara National Park**, where the dry forests of the north meet the humid forests of the south, with species from both habitats appearing in the reserve. The forests include some rare hardwood trees, while the extensive bird list includes endangered species such as the scarlet macaw. Boat trips can be arranged along the Río Tárcoles and a wide range of water birds can be spotted, including a variety of herons, pelicans, anhingas and kingfishers. There is also a large egret roost.

The road south from Carara, sometimes marked on maps as the **Costanera Sur**, has deteriorated in recent years. It reaches the town of **Jacó**, the nearest beach resort to San José and by Costa Rican standards quite lively. The beach, which stretches for 3km (1.5 miles), is disappointing. The water is often polluted and rip tides are a problem for swimmers. There is excellent surfing, however, especially on the beaches south of the town. Jacó has a single main street running parallel to the beach, lined with hotels, boutiques, restaurants and discos.

The Costañera continues south through ranching country, with side roads leading to remote beaches, many with excellent surf. On the approach to **Parrita**, oil palms

Right: *Male iguanas can grow to nearly 2m (6ft) in length.*

Opposite above:
Previously an important banana exporting port, Quepos is now the main sportfishing centre on the Pacific coast.

Opposite below: *Old buses take quite a pounding on the rough roads in the region around Quepos.*

dominate. Small settlements appear at regular intervals among plantations, each with identical houses clustered around a soccer field; one-way bridges lead across streams. This pattern is repeated until Quepos is reached.

Quepos

Named after the *Quepoa* Indian tribe who originally inhabited the area, Quepos used to be a banana exporting port, but disease wiped out the banana crop. Decline then set in, but the town's fortunes have revived with the recent growth of tourism and its close proximity to the Manuel Antonio National Park, some 7km (4 miles) to the south. **White-water rafting** is popular on the nearby Río Naranjo, while the town is also becoming a major **sportfishing** centre, with sailfish and marlin the main targets. Quepos has plenty of accommodation, mainly in the budget range, but with its decaying banana docks and dilapidated air, there is little to stimulate the visitor.

A road runs inland and then parallel to the shore for 7km (4 miles) to the village of **Manuel Antonio**. The road is lined with various hotels and restaurants, all with superb jungle and ocean views. There is also a loop at the end of the road alongside Playa Espadilla; this is backed with bars, restaurants and shops.

SURF'S UP!

Costa Rica's waves are renowned throughout the surfing world. The best beach on the **Caribbean** coast is at Puerto Viejo, with its famed *La Salsa Brava* wave. There is good surfing along the full length of the **Pacific** coast, with the best spots at Playa Naranjo in the Santa Rosa National Park, Playa Grande near Tamarindo, Manuel Antonio and Dominical. The best of all, however, is undoubtedly at Pavones, a surfers' Mecca, reputedly sporting the longest wave in the world, which if conditions are right, can give a 1km, three minute ride! For news on surfing, call the 24-hour **Surf Report Hotline**, tel: 233-7386.

THE CERRO DE MUERTE

One of the most perilous
stretches of road in Costa
Rica is on the Interamericana,
100km (62 miles) south of
San José, where the road
runs over the 3491m
(11,450ft) pass known as the
Cerro de Muerte or 'hill of
death'. The road at this point
has a number of hairpin
bends and deep potholes and
is frequently affected by mud
and rock slides. Clouds make
visibility poor and the large
trucks which use the road
are themselves poorly lit.
Accidents are common, as
the roadside crosses testify.
Avoid the Cerro de Muerte if
possible, particularly at night.

Below: *Beautiful Manuel
Antonio is with good reason
the country's most popular
national park.*
Opposite: *Many wealthy
Ticos own a second home
on the beach, such as this
one at Dominical.*

Manuel Antonio National Park ★★★

Although it is the smallest of Costa Rica's national parks,
covering a mere 683ha (1688 acres), Manuel Antonio is
the most popular in terms of visitor numbers, with
around 150,000 annually. Because of overuse, there is
now a limit of 600 visitors daily and the reserve is closed
on Mondays. Its attraction is not difficult to appreciate.
The hill slopes are covered with dense **humid tropical
forest**, while rocky headlands are interspersed with cres-
cent-shaped coral sand beaches. A low sandy spit links
with a former island, which ends at a headland known
as **Cathedral Point**. There are a number of short trails,
the most popular of which circumnavigates Cathedral
Point, while another leads up to a viewpoint. This is one
of the few places in Costa Rica where all four varieties of
monkeys can be seen, including the endangered squirrel
monkey, while bathers on the beaches may be pestered
by scavenging white-faced monkeys. Other mammals
include sloths, agoutis, coatis, armadillos and racoons,
while 350 species of birds have been recorded. Many visitors, however, see more wildlife on the less used forest
trails around their hotels. The park is open from 07:00 to
17:00 Tuesday to Sunday and is entered by wading
through a shallow tidal stream at the south end of the
public beach. Arrive prepared for rain – the park averages 3800mm (150in) annually and even the dry season
is not totally rainless.

Dominical and San Isidro

To continue south from Manual Antonio, it is necessary to return to Quepos and take the bumpy gravel road that runs for 45km (28 miles) to **Dominical** through more African palm plantations. Dominical, once a quiet fishing village, was undiscovered until recently. Now sportfishing, surfing and snorkelling are attracting an increasing number of visitors. Approximately 1km (0.5 mile) north of Dominical is the private nature reserve of **Hacienda Barú**. It has a variety of habitats including mangroves, pasture and primary rainforest, plus a turtle nesting beach. In the other direction is the **Marino Ballena National Park**, which includes the Uvita tombolo, numerous beaches, mangroves and the largest coral reef on the Pacific coast. The beaches are home to green iguanas which graze on the algae in the salt water pools, while the island contains breeding colonies of blue-footed boobies and magnificent frigate birds. The park gets its name from the *ballenas* or hump-backed whales which migrate past the point from December to March. Dolphins are seen all year round.

CLIMBING MOUNT CHIRRIPÓ

There are clearly marked walking trails to the summit of Costa Rica's highest peak and mountaineering skills are not required. Climbs begin at the National Park's ranger station in the village of **San Gerardo de Rivas**, which is at a height of 1350m (4430ft). The summit is at 3820m (12,533ft), making it a climb of 2470m! Not to be taken lightly, the climb to the summit and back can be completed in two days, but most people take three, staying overnight in the huts available on the route, which can cope with up to 50 people. Warm clothing is needed as temperatures near the summit drop below freezing point at night.

A welcoming paved road runs northeast from Dominical through the deep winding valley of the Río Barú and into the Fila Costeña mountains, eventually reaching **San Isidro de El General**. This is the most important town on the southern part of the Interamericana, as well as being the gateway to the **Valle de El General**. To the north, the Interamericana runs over the **Cerro de la Muerte** pass, which at 3491m (11,450ft) is the highest road in the country. A minor road heads northeast from San Isidro to the village of **San Gerardo de Rivas**, where the ranger station marks the boundary of the **Chirripó National Park**. The village is the starting point of treks to the summit of **Mount Chirripó**, the highest mountain peak in Costa Rica.

Above: *The Boruca Indian Reserve, with its small police station, is one of 22 such reserves in the country.*
Opposite: *South of Palmar Norte, the Río Sierpe flows towards the Pacific.*

The Southern Pacific Lowlands

Southeast from San Isidro the Interamericana runs through the Valle de El General, which although lacking volcanic soil, is fertile enough to have a thriving agricultural industry, based on pineapples and coffee. There is a **Boruca Indian Reserve** in the south of the valley, where wooden and textile handicrafts can be bought.

The Interamericana then swings through the Fila Costeña coastal range of mountains along the deep Grande de Térraba valley and enters the coastal lowlands at **Palmar Norte**. The town is both the service centre for the local banana industry and the gateway to the Osa Peninsula and Golfo Dulce. Just to the south of Palmar is the **Valle de Diquis**, famous for its numerous and controversial **lithic spheres**.

THE DIQUIS

Of all the *indigenas* groups of pre-Columbian Costa Rica, the Diquis are perhaps the most remarkable. From their homeland in the northern part of the Osa Peninsula, they fashioned the **gold** jewellery which so excited Columbus. It is possible that they were also responsible for the **lithic spheres** found throughout the southwest of the country. How they were able to make these large granite spheres, and take them to the Isla de Caño some 22km (14 miles) offshore, still excites debate.

OSA PENINSULA

Second only to the Nicoya Peninsula in size, Osa, which boasts one of the largest remaining areas of coastal rain forest in Central America, stretches for 60km (37 miles) between the Pacific Ocean and the Golfo Dulce. The whole peninsula has a frontier atmosphere about it, with redundant banana workers attempting to establish small holdings or trying their luck at panning for gold. The area has been 'discovered' as a tourist venue in recent years and, despite its remoteness, it is popular with young backpackers for hikes and forest trekking, while more affluent visitors stay in the recently opened wildlife and sportfishing lodges.

The only decent road on the peninsula runs down the eastern side to **Puerto Jiménez**, a small settlement of around 6000 people and the gateway to the Corcovado National Park, which has an office in the town. Puerto Jímenez has plenty of clean, basic accommodation, some restaurants, and several good surfing and swimming beaches to the south of the town. Tourism is a burgeoning industry here and there are a number of organizations providing exciting adventure trips, such as kayaking and forest trekking. SANSA runs daily flights from San José via Golfito.

GOLD IN THE PARK

The gold industry revived in the 1980s in Costa Rica. Many of the gold miners or *oreros* were banana workers made redundant when United Fruit closed down in 1985. When the Corcovado Park was set up, there were thousands of *oreros* working within park's boundaries, causing damage. They were evicted and promised compensation. However, this was slow to materialize and protests ensued. At the moment there is an uneasy truce.

Above: *The enormous Golfo Dulce is fringed by swamplands, forested areas and remote beaches.*

WORKING (OR NOT WORKING) FOR THE YUNAI

When **Minor Keith** built the Jungle Railway, he financed the last stretch by planting bananas along the trackside. The fruit became a major export, employing Jamaican railway workers. Keith formed the **United Fruit Company** (the *Yunai*), which was to have a profound sociological influence. On the plus side, the *Yunai* took a paternal interest in its workers, providing houses, schools and hospitals, while its workers were relatively well paid. On the debit side, it employed anti-union practices and would desert an area if faced with trouble. After strikes in the 1930s, it moved to the Pacific coast. The **United Brands**, as it is now known, then closed its banana operations in 1985, when disease hit the crop, replacing them with less labour-intensive oil palms.

Corcovado National Park ★★

Formed in 1975 and covering approximately 42,000ha (104,000 acres) of primary forest, Corcovado is undoubtedly the most beautiful and remote of Costa Rica's national parks. It protects endangered species such as the scarlet macaw, harpy eagle, squirrel monkey and jaguar, while four species of sea turtle breed on the park's beaches. The vegetation has been compared with the Amazon and the 500 species of trees often reach an immense height, with huge buttress roots.

With over 400 species of birds, 139 mammals and over 100 types of amphibians and reptiles, there is plenty for the visitor to see. Trekking in the Corcovado is not without its hazards, however. Rainfall averages 4000mm (158in) a year and insects are persistent, while herds of aggressive peccaries, crocodiles, snakes and sharks can be a threat. Despite, or perhaps because of, these obstacles, Corcovado is becoming popular for those seeking a wilderness experience. The trails should be entered via the peripheral ranger stations and the park fees can be paid there or at the information office in Puerto Jiménez.

Another increasingly visited spot on the Osa Peninsula is **Bahía Drake** in the northwest. Pronounced DRA-kay, it was named after Sir Francis Drake, who stopped off at the Bay in 1579 during his circumnavigation of the world aboard the *Golden Hind*. The small village of **Agujitas** straggles around the Bay, which is a favourite port-of-call for yachtsmen. The local lodges run tours to the Corcovado National Park, and arrange sportfishing and horseriding. Lying 17km (10.6 miles) off-shore is the **Isla del Caño Biological Reserve**, which has some marvellous coral reefs. There are also a number of **lithic spheres** to be seen, apparently brought there by the Diquis *indígenas* people.

GOLFITO AREA

The **Golfo Dulce** is a large bay between the Osa Peninsula and the Fila Costeña mountains to the northeast. The narrow coastal plain is mainly taken up by bananas and oil palms, before merging into the slim, largely uninhabited strip of the Peninsula de Burica.

Golfito

The town is located on a small bay on the northeast side of the Golfo Dulce. It was set up when the United Fruit Company moved its headquarters here in 1938 and it became an important banana exporting port. Golfito straggles on either side of a single road along the shore, leading northwards to the superior *zona americana*, where the Fruit Company's executives lived, and southwards to the more scruffy and people-intensive *pueblo civil*. When United pulled out in 1985, decline set in and Golfito now has a run-down look about it. However, tourism is slowly beginning to take off and the latest government has given the town a further boost by making it a 'duty free' port. To take advantage of this, buyers have to spend 24 hours in the town, which means that the hotels are often full.

> **WILSON BOTANICAL GARDENS**
>
> Located 6km (4 miles) south of San Vito, these gardens were set up by Robert and Catherine Wilson in 1963. As well as cultivated gardens there is an adjacent reserve. Over 10km (6 miles) of trails run through the gardens, which have some 2000 species of plants, including orchids, bamboos, tree ferns, palms and bromeliads. Open Tuesday–Sunday 08:00–16:00.

Below: *Since the United Fruit Company moved out, the Golfito area has come increasingly to rely on tourism, helped by Golfito's status as a duty free port; nevertheless, some agriculture continues to take place.*

PARQUE INTERNACIONAL LA AMISTAD

This international **'friendship park'** straddles the border between Costa Rica and Panama. A **World Heritage Site**, it includes nine distinct **life zones** and its diverse vegetation supports a wide variety of wildlife. There is no accommodation within the park and access is difficult, making this a destination for only experienced hikers.

Below: *Coco Island is said to have buried treasure that remains unclaimed.*

So far the town itself has little else of interest, but makes a good base for exploring the surrounding area. In the background are the forest-covered hills of the **Golfito National Wildlife Refuge**. There are a couple of marinas to the south of the town and sportfishing is becoming increasingly important.

Two hours drive south of Golfito is the surfing Mecca of **Playa Pavones**, which is reputed to have the longest continuous wave in the world. Surfing conditions are best during the rainy season from May to October. Accommodation in Pavones is mainly in simple *cabinas* and surf boards can be rented.

ISLA DEL COCO NATIONAL PARK *

The Isla del Coco lies over 500km (312 miles) southwest of Costa Rica, and at 24km^2 (9 sq miles), is claimed to be the largest uninhabited island in the world. However, there have been numerous unsuccessful attempts in the past to colonize the island, and the feral populations of domestic animals which now remain, such as goats, pigs and cats, pose a threat to the indigenous wildlife. Because of its isolated position it has a number of endemic animals and plants. It also boasts extensive pristine coral reef. There is talk of a secret treasure, supposed to be buried on the island, but yet to be found.

The Southern Pacific Coast at a Glance

Best Times To Visit

The north has a pronounced **dry season** between December and March, but rainfall totals in the remainder of the year are low. The south has rain throughout the year.

Getting There

Access to the north of the region is easy, with good **roads** to Puntarenas. Roads are poor in the south and most visitors **fly** from San José to the airstrips at Golfito, Puerto Jiménez and Palmar.

Getting Around

Road communictions are reasonable in the north. In the south, the Interamericana runs through to the Panama border, but elsewhere roads are poor. A **passenger ferry** runs daily from Golfito to Puerto Jiménez.

Where to Stay

Luxury
Villa Caletas, Tárcoles, Apdo.12358-1000, tel: 257-3653, fax: 222-2059. Breath-taking hilltop location.
Hotel Si Como No, Manuel Antonio, tel: 777-1250, fax: 777-1093. Eco-friendly, award-winning architecture.
Hotel Fiesta, Apdo.171, Puntarenas 5400, tel: 239-4266, fax: 239-0217. Resort complex with casino.
Hotel Hacienda Lilipoza, Apdo.15, Jacó 4023, tel: 643-3062, fax: 643-3158. Hacienda-style units.

Mid-range
Hotel Costa Verde, Manuel Antonio, Apdo.89 Escazú, tel: 777-0584, fax: 777-0560. Apartments with sea views.
Hotel Río Lindo, Dominical, tel: 771-2009, fax: 771-1725. New hotel with pool.
Las Gaviotas, Pueblo Civil, Golfito, tel: 775-0062, fax: 775-0544. Waterside hotel, with private moorings.
Tiskita Lodge, Bahía Pavones, tel: 233-6890, fax: 255-4410. Rustic, beach-side cabins, with nearby trails.
Casa Corcovado, Drake Bay Osa Peninsula, tel: 256-3181, fax:256-7409. Deluxe jungle lodge next to National Park. Bar, pool, and wildlife.

Budget
Los Ranchos, Playa Jacó, tel and fax: 643-3070. Cabinas around a pool.
Cabinas Piscis, Playa Espadilla, Manuel Antonio, Apdo.207 Quepos, tel: 777-0046. Basic accommodation, near beach.

Where to Eat

Posada del Descanso, San Gerardo de Rivas (no phone). Ideal base from which to climb Mount Chirripó.
La Pirámide Restaurant, Golfito, tel: 775-0131.
Gourmet food in style.
Plinios, Quepos, tel: 777-0055. Italian food and superb buffet breakfast.
Barba Roja, Manuel Antonio, tel: 777-0331. Outdoor dining with seafood specialities.
El Bosque, on main road south of Jacó, tel: 643-3009. Seafood under mango trees.
Steve and Lisa's Paradise Cove, Playa Malo, Tárcoles, tel: 228-9430. Beach views.
Bar Mar Marina Restaurant, Puntarenas, tel: 661-3064. Serves Costa Rican seafood.

Tours and Excursions

In the north, the most popular tours are to **Tortuga Island**, **Iguana Park** and the **Carara National Park**. The National Park at **Manuel Antonio** is superb. In the south, wildlife fans can visit the **Corcovado** National Park.

Useful Contacts

ICT, tel: 661-1985.
For domestic flights to the south of the region contact: **SANSA**, tel: 221-9414.
Travelair, tel: 232-7883.
For park information contact: **Servicio de Parques Nacionales (SPN)**, tel: 257-0922.

PUNTARENAS	J	F	M	A	M	J	J	A	S	O	N	D
AVERAGE TEMP. °F	82	84	86	82	82	82	81	81	81	81	81	82
AVERAGE TEMP. °C	28	29	30	30	28	28	28	27	27	27	27	28
RAINFALL in	0.02	0.02	0.4	0.8	4.5	7.1	6.9	6.1	8.9	8.1	3.5	0.8
RAINFALL mm	0.5	0.5	10	20	115	180	175	155	225	205	90	20

Travel Tips

Tourist Information

The Costa Rican Tourist Board, the **Instituto Costarricense de Turismo (ICT)**, Plaza de la Cultura, San José, tel: 222-1090, fax: 223-5452, provides maps and other information for the traveller in English. The address for letters is Apartado Postal (777) 1000. ICT do not have branches abroad, but information can be obtained from consulates. The only other ICT offices within Costa Rica are at Juan Santamaría Airport and at the Peñas Blanca border crossing with Nicaragua, although there are plans to set up regional branches. There are locally run initiatives in some of the smaller towns. In the US, the **Costa Rican Brochure Service** can provide booklets and information, tel: (8000) 327-7033.

Entry Requirements

A passport is required for all visitors. Citizens of the US, UK, Canada and most EU countries are granted a 90-day entry stamp. Citizens of Ireland, France, Australia and New Zealand are allowed to stay for 30 days. Most other nationalities need a visa, which can be obtained from Costa Rican consulates at around US$20. Visitors wishing to stay longer can apply for an extension, but, as this can be a time-consuming process, it is wiser to leave the country for 72 hours by crossing the border into Nicaragua or Panama and then obtain a re-entry stamp.

Customs

Visitors to Costa Rica are allowed to bring in 3 litres of wine or spirits, 500 cigarettes (or 500g of tobacco) and 6 rolls of film (although this is rarely checked). There is usually no problem with sporting gear and other equipment. An airport tax of approximately US$17 is payable on all international flights leaving from Costa Rica, either in *colones* or US dollars.

Health Requirements

Although vaccinations are not mandatory for Costa Rica, it is wise for visitors to make sure that their polio, typhoid, hepatitis and tetanus jabs are all up-to-date before setting off. Visitors spending time in the rain forest areas should take a course of prophylactics.

CONVERSION CHART		
FROM	**TO**	**MULTIPLY BY**
Millimetres	Inches	0.0394
Metres	Yards	1.0936
Metres	Feet	3.281
Kilometres	Miles	0.6214
Kilometres square	Square miles	0.386
Hectares	Acres	2.471
Litres	Pints	1.760
Kilograms	Pounds	2.205
Tonnes	Tons	0.984

To convert Celsius to Fahrenheit: $x \times 9 \div 5 + 32$

Getting There

Costa Rica can be reached by air, road and boat.

By Air: The main point of entry is San José's Juan Santamaría international airport, situated about 16km (10 miles) from the city. A new international airport has been built at Liberia to cater for the holiday resorts of the Nicoya Peninsula, but receives few flights, as yet. Most of the airlines serving Costa Rica are American. **Continental** fly via Houston and Newark **United** fly daily direct to San José from Washington DC, Los Angeles and Chicago; **American Airlines** fly via Miami and Dallas; **Delta** also fly from the US. From Europe, connections can be made through US cities, try **Iberia** via Madrid, **Condor** from Germany, and **Martinair** via Amsterdam. The Costa Rican carrier, **Lacsa** (tel: (800) 296-0909), connects with a number of US cities. **APEX** fares are the cheapest, but some restrictions are imposed.

By Road: It is possible for US citizens to drive to Costa Rica, but this is not a popular option. It is 4000km (2500 miles) from the US border to San José through several countries, many regarded as unsafe, while border delays can be expected and the paper work is challenging. Buses run from Panama City in Panama and Managua in Nicaragua, to the city of San José. Both services take around 12 hours. Services are run by two companies: **Tica Bus** (tel: (506) 221-8954) and **Sirca** (tel: (506) 222-5541).

By Water: A large number of cruise ships visit Costa Rica, mainly calling at Puerto Limón on the Caribbean coast and Puerto Caldera on the Pacific side of the country. It is also possible to enter Costa Rica by river boat along the Río San Juan, which forms the border with Nicaragua, disembarking at San Carlos.

USEFUL PHRASES

Yes, No • *Sí, No*
Please, Thank You •
Por favor, Gracias
Hello, Goodbye •
Hola, Adiós
See you later • *Hasta luego*
My name is ... • *Me llamo ...*
Do you speak English? •
¿Habla (usted) inglés?
You're welcome • *De nada*
I don't speak Spanish •
No hablo español
How much is...? •
¿Cuánto cuesta...?
Do you have...? • *¿Tiene...?*
Please speak more slowly •
*Hable más despacio,
por favor*
Where is...? •
¿Dónde está...?
What time does it
leave/arrive? •
¿A qué hora sale/llega?
It's too expensive •
Es demasiado caro
Do you have anything
cheaper? •
¿No tiene algo más barato?
Is there...? • *¿Hay...?*
Please fill the tank •
Llénelo del todo, por favor
Is there a hotel near here? •
¿Hay un hotel por aquí?

Sadly, the scenic 'Jungle Railway' from Puerto Limón to San José was closed in 1991 after earthquake damage.

What to Pack

As in all tropical countries, light clothing is advisable, particularly items which can be easily washed and dried. San José and the Central Valley, however, can be cool at night, so that a light jumper is often needed. A hat offers protection from both the harsh sun and the rain. Rainwear, too, is highly recommended, particularly when visiting the cloud forest regions. As rainwear can cause sweat in the humidity, visitors may prefer a collapsible umbrella. Rain forest outings require long sleeves, trousers and rubber boots. Beachwear should be confined to the beach and shorts are out-of-place in San José. Topless bathing and nudity are unacceptable to Costa Ricans and will cause offence. Smart casual wear is suitable in most hotels. Useful items for any traveller include a pocket torch; travel alarm clock; ear plugs; sun block; insect repellent and a first aid kit. Few visitors will be without binoculars and camera. Many people use San José as a base for travelling around the country and it is quite normal to leave part of your luggage in the storeroom of your hotel and pick it up on your return.

Money Matters

Currency: The central unit of currency in Costa Rica is the *colón*, plural *colones*, named after Cristóbal Colón (Columbus) and divided into 100 *centimos*. There are coins of 1, 5, 10, 20, 25, 50 100 and 500 *colones*, and notes of 500, 1000, 5000 and 10,000 *colones*. Because of the high rate of inflation, *centimos* are rarely encountered and are being phased out. At the time of writing there are approximately 340 *colones* to the UK£ and around 317 *colones* to the US$, but bear in mind that the Central Bank devalues the *colón* at a rate of around 0.10 a day, which is specifically designed to keep the currency consistent with the value of the dollar and keep inflation down.

ROAD SIGNS

Traffic signs are generally inadequate and do not always follow internationally recognized traffic symbols.
Adelante • Ahead
Alto • Stop
Ceda el Paso • Give Way
Curva Peligrosa •
Dangerous Curve
Derrumbes/Desprendimientos en la Via • Rockfalls on the road
Despacio • Slow
Desvio • Detour
Mantenga Su Derecha •
Keep to the Right
No Adelantar • No Passing
No Estacionar • No Parking
Prohibido el Paso/No Hay Paso • No Entrance
Peligro • Danger
Trabajos en la Via •
Roadworks

Colones are almost impossible to obtain abroad and visitors are therefore advised to bring to Costa Rica a mixture of US traveller's cheques and US cash, both of which are widely accepted.

Traveller's Cheques: Should be bought in US$ only. Traveller's cheques can only be used as cash in the higher grade hotels. Cash and traveller's cheques are readily exchanged in banks and the larger hotels, but be prepared for long waits in banks. Hotels will make a larger service charge than banks, but at least queues will be avoided.

Credit Cards: Visa and Mastercard are widely accepted, AmEx less so. Smaller restaurants and hotels may only accept cash, as will most petrol stations. Most private banks will give advances on credit cards. Many restaurants and shops add an additional charge to credit card transactions, which may be as high as 10%.

Banking Hours: May vary slightly from branch to branch and region to region, but are usually Mon–Fri 09:00–15:00. Closed Sat.

Taxes: There is a sales tax of 13% in restaurants, plus a service charge of 10%, which can be quite a shock when the bill arrives. Hotels charge 16.39% tax.

Tipping: You need not tip a taxi driver, but a hotel porter generally expects something. In restaurants, the service charge is automatically put on the bill. Tourist guides should normally be tipped.

Accommodation

The best accommodation in Costa Rica goes under the heading of '**hotels**', but there are few in the international luxury category, except in San José or on the Pacific coast. Two new, all-embracing resorts have been built at Playa Tambor and Papagayo which clearly breach Costa Rica's green approach to tourism. There are a number of 'boutique hotels', usually located in old colonial houses. Below the hotel classification, comes accommodation with names such as *hostales*, *hospejades*, *pensiones* and *posadas*. At the budget end of the scale there are *cabinas*, appealing mainly to back-packers and *tico* families at weekends. There is a small network of 10 **youth hostels**, often located in, or near, national parks. Avoid 'motels', which are usually little more than brothels.

Eco-lodges are usually found in national parks, rain forests and remote locations. Facilities are generally spartan and visitors should be prepared to share with insects and other small creatures.

Camp sites are widespread throughout Costa Rica, particularly in national parks and on the Pacific coast. Reserve accommodation well ahead during the high season. As few accommodations outside San José have recognizable addresses, it is easier to reserve a place with a credit card by fax. Once in Costa Rica, confirm the booking by telephone.

Eating Out

Whilst local cuisine is generally uninspiring, international restaurants are common in San José, with French, Japanese, Italian and Spanish food readily available. Away from the capital, the choice becomes more limited and in some areas the hotel dining room may be the only option. For cheap food, try the *sodas*, which are similar to US diners. The *plato del día* (dish of the day) is usually a bargain. Restaurants often close by 22:00, and the 10% service charge and 13% sales tax on all meals will not appear on the menu price.

Transport

Air: There are two domestic airlines in Costa Rica – **Sansa** and **Travelair**. **Sansa** (tel: 221-9414) is state-owned and notoriously inefficient. It operates twin-engined DC3s from Juan Santamaría Airport. Its rival, **Travelair**, is more expensive, but provides a better service. It operates Britten Islander aircraft from Tobías Bolaños Airport at Pavas. Small groups of people may also charter aircraft quite cheaply. This can be arranged through travel agents.

Road: Visitors driving in Costa Rica need a valid foreign driving licence or an International Driving Permit. **Car Rental** should only be considered as a last resort. If you are willing to take on the hazards of the roads, it is best to rent though a travel agent, who will take responsibility for any problems which may occur. Drivers need to be over 21

(some rental agencies make this 23) and have a credit card in their name. Car rental agencies, ICT and the airport will provide road maps.

Buses: This is the cheapest way of getting around Costa Rica. The ICT office in San José can provide up-to-date listings on destinations.

Taxis: In San José, taxis are numerous and cheap. They are red, with a yellow triangle on the door. Make sure that the meter (*maría*) is switched on at the start of the journey. In rural areas, taxis are often 4WD Jeeps, but will also be red with a yellow triangle.

Business Hours

Banks normally open Mon–Fri 09:00–15:00; offices are open 08:00–17:00 and shops and stores 09:00–18:00. All shops are likely to close between noon and 14:00. Most shops open on Saturdays, but close on Sundays.

Communications

The Costa Rican postal system, Correos de Costa Rica, is fairly efficient, but expect delays if posting mail from rural areas. Even small settlements will have a post office (*correo*) and a *lista de correo* or poste restante service. Although **telephone calls** within Costa Rica are cheap, long distance calls can be expensive. The cheapest periods are between 20:00 and 07:00 and at weekends. The country code for Costa Rica is 506. All numbers have seven digits and there are no area codes. For information, dial 113.

HOLIDAYS AND FESTIVALS

As Costa Rica is a Roman Catholic country, many of the holidays are related to the church. On important holidays, hotels are likely to be fully booked.

January 1 •
New Year's Day *Año Nuevo*

March 19 •
St. Joseph's Day
Día de San José

Movable date •
Easter Week
Semana Santa

April 11 •
Juan Santamaría Day
Día de Juan Santamaría
(Day of the national hero)

May 1 •
Labour Day *Día del Trabajo*

June 29 •
Sts Peter and Paul Day
Día de San Pedro y San Pablo
(Processions in villages of those names)

Mid July •
Fiesta of the Virgin of the Sea
Fiesta de la Virgen del Mar

July 25 •
Annexation of Guanacaste
Día de Guanacaste
(Celebrates the province becoming part of Costa Rica)

August 2 •
Virgin of Los Angeles Day
Día de Virgen de los Ángeles

August 15 •
Mothers' Day *Día del Madre*

September 15 •
Independence Day
Día de la Independencia

October 12 •
Columbus Day
Día de la Raza

December 8 •
Immaculate Conception of the Virgin Mary
Inmaculada Concepción

December 25 •
Christmas Day *Navidad*
(Celebrations continue until **January 2**)

Time difference

Costa Rica is 6 hrs behind GMT and in North America's Standard time zone.

Electricity

The electrical supply is 110 volts, the same as in US and Canada. Visitors from Europe, Australia and other countries using 240 volts will need to travel with an adaptor.

Health Precautions

To guard against **sunburn**, use a high factor sun screen and wear a sun hat, even on overcast days. The heat can also lead to **dehydration**, which is a particular problem for hikers in the hotter western side of the country. Keep up a high fluid intake and have rehydration salts handy. The heat and sun can also lead to **diarrhoea**. Bring a non-prescription remedy. **Water** is generally safe to drink, but in some remote regions it might be prudent to use bottled water. **Malaria** is only a problem in the Caribbean lowlands. The malaria-carrying mosquitoes are only active at night, so use a mosquito net or burn coils. **Dengue fever**, on the other hand, is caused by day-flying mosquitoes, so be aware and use an insect repellent. Many people say that vitamin B tablets help to prevent mosquito bites. A **first aid kit** with relevant prescription medicines is a vital luggage item. Before you set out, ensure that your travel insurance covers all possible medical emergencies.

Health Services

Public hospitals provide a free service to all, including foreigners. If a private clinic is used, the doctor will expect to be paid immediately, leaving the visitor to be reimbursed by the insurance company.

Personal Safety

Elementary precautions should be taken to avoid opportunistic crime. Be particularly wary in downtown San José, Puerto Limón and Puntarenas where pickpockets operate. Use a concealed body pouch. Have a copy made of your passport. Leave valuables in the hotel safe. Hired cars are easily recognized and therefore prime targets. Park vehicles in a safe compound at night. The general emergency telephone number is 911. Any tourist related crime should be reported to ICT.

Etiquette

It is a natural part of Costa Rican culture to be polite, friendly and responsible. *Ticos* like to leave a good impression. Dress, therefore, tends to be formal, particularly in towns and in business situations. Shorts are out of place in San José. On meeting, both sexes tend to shake hands and men and women may kiss each other on the cheek.

Language

The official language of Costa Rica is Spanish, although some Indian languages are still spoken in isolated areas. English is spoken relatively widely in the tourist-related industries, but a little knowledge of Spanish is helpful for the visitor and will naturally delight *ticos*. Bring a phrasebook and a Spanish dictionary.

GOOD READING

Visitors interested in wildlife in general, and birds in particular, will need good field guides:
- F.G. Stiles and A.F. Skutch (1989) *Guide to the Birds of Costa Rica*, Cornell University Press. The bird watchers' bible, but expensive.
- Philip de Vries (1987) *The Butterflies of Costa Rica*, Princton University Press. Comprehensive guide for keen lepidopterists.
- Daniel H. Janzen (1983) *Costa Rican Natural History*, University of Chicago Press. Definitive work, for reference rather than field use.

- Mario A. Boza (1988) *Costa Rica National Parks*, Heliconia. Coffee-table book, with wonderful photographs. Other general books include:
- Edelman and Kenen (1989) *The Costa Rica Reader*, Grove Press. A set of essays on the history, sociology and politics of the country.
- Richard, Karen and Mavis Biesanz (1987) *The Costa Ricans*, Prentice Hall. Politics and culture of Costa Rica.
- Carmen Naranjo, *There Never Was Once Upon a Time: A Collection of Stories from Costa Rica's Best Known Fiction Writers*.

INDEX

Note: Numbers in **bold** indicate photographs

aerial tram **52**
Afro-Caribbeans 61, 72
agoutis 79, 106, 114
Aguas Zarcas 79
Agujitas 118
Alajuela 18, 45, 46-47
Alfaro, Anastasio 57
Amón 40
anteaters 11
Arenal Botanical Gardens 83
Arenal National Park 81
Arenal Observatory Lodge 80
armadillos 11, 64, 79, 97, 114
arribadas 103
Asociación Talamanqueña de Ecoturismo y Conservación (ATEC) 66
Atenas 45, 110
Aviarios del Caribe Wildlife Sanctuary 65

Bagaces 94
Bahia de Culebra 100
Bahia Drake 118
Balneario Tabacón 81
Barra del Colorado 15, 67, 71, **72**, 84
Barra del Colorado National Wildlife Refuge 61
Barra Honda National Park 99
Barva 50, **51**
Basílica de la Inmaculada Concepción 50
Basílica de Nuestra Señora de los Angeles **53**
basilisks 12, 79, 84
bats 11, 99
Bien, Amos 77
birds 13, **15**, 47, 52, 54, 55, 58, 65, 66, 69, 72, 77, 78, 83, 84, 86, 93, 97, 102, 106, 112, 114, 118
bocas 30, **31**
Boruca Indian Reserve **116**
Botos Lake **49**
Braulio Carrillo National Park 52, 62, 76
Bribri, the 25, 51, 61, 66
bullfighting 27
butterflies **13**, 52, 54, 70, **71**, 78, 83, 86, 88, **106**

C.A.T.I.E. (see Centro Agrónomo Tropical de

Investigación y Enseñanza)
C.A.S.E.M. 88
Cabécar, the 61
Café Britt 50
Cahuita 61, 64
Cahuita National Park 8, 64, **65**
Caldera 110, 111
Cañas 93
Caño Negro Wildlife Refuge 75, 80, **84**
Caño Palma Biological Station 69
canopy tours 88
Carara National Park 112
Cartago 18, 45, 53
Casa Amarilla **37**
Casa de la Cultura 110
Cascada La Paz 49
Catedral Metropolitana 37
Catholicism (see Roman Catholicism)
cattle 45, 75, **78**, 91
Central Market, San José **29**
Centro Agrónomo Tropical de Investigación y Enseñanza 57
ceramics 26, **48**, **98**
Cerro Chirripó (see Mt Chirripó)
Cerro de la Muerte 109, 116
Cerro Tortuguero 71
Chapel of the Holy Sacrament 37
Chirripó National Park 116
Chorotegas, the 93, 98
Church of San Blas 99
Church of San José de Orosi 55
Ciudad Blanca (see Liberia)
Ciudad Quesada **79**
climate 9
coatis 79, 93, 114
Cóbano 105
coconut 31
Cocos Plate 6
coffee **22**, 31, 51
colonial architecture 94
Columbus, Christopher **17**, 18
coral reefs 8, 64, 66
Corcovado 109
Cordillera Central 6, 45, 61, 62, 75, 76, 79
Cordillera de Guanacaste 6, 91
Cordillera de Talamanca 7, 45, 55, 61
Cordillera de Tilarán 6, 85, 91

Coronado 51
Costanera Sur 112
Creole cooking 29, 61, 65
crocodiles 111, 118
Curú National Wildlife Refuge 104

Daniel Oduber Quiros International Airport 95
Diego de la Haya crater 56
dolphins 15, 115
Dominical **115**

eco-lodges 15, **23**, 75, 76
eco-tourism 15
Ecomuseo de las Minas de Abangares 92
economy 22
Edificio Metálico 37
education 23, 24
El Fortin tower **50**
El Plástico 78
El Tucano Country Club 79
elections **20**, 22
epiphytes 11, 54, 86

Feria del Ganado 79
Fernández, Juan Mora 19
festivals 19
Figueras, José María 21
Fila de Bustamente 109
flag 29
folk dancing 98
food 28
Fortuna 75, **81**

Gandoca-Manzanillo Wildlife Refuge 64, 66
Grecia **47**
gold 117
Golfito 15, **119**
Golfito National Wildlife Refuge 120
Golfo Dulce 117, **118**
government 22
Grecia 47, 48
Guácimo 62
Guanacaste National Park 96, 97
Guápiles 62, 76
Guápiles Highway 61, 62
Guaitil 98
Guayabo **58**

Hacienda Barú 115
Hamburgo de Siquirres 67
health services 126
Heredia 45, 50
hiking 28
history 16-21
horse riding 28, 78, 79
hotels 42, 59, 73, 89, 107, 121, 124

Hummingbird Gallery 88
hummingbirds 14, 15, 70, **88**

ICT (see Tourist Information Office)
Iglesia la Agonia 46
Iguana Park 111
iguanas 12, 72, 84, **112**, 115
indigenas 24, 25, 39, 61, 64, 72
International Children's Rainforest 86
International Sportfishing Tournament 101
Isla de los Pájaros 93
Isla del Caño Biological Reserve 118
Isla del Coco 8, 64, **120**
Isla del Coco National Park 120
Isla Tortuga 104

Jacó 109, 112
Jade Museum 37, 38, **39**
Janzen, David 97
jewellery 26
Juan Santamaria Cultural-Historical Museum 46
Juan Santamaria Park 46
jungle lodges 67, 69
Jungle Railway 20, 24, 61, 62, 110
Juntas 92

kayaking 117
Keith, Minor 20, 61, 118
KeköLdi Reserve 66

La Agonia 94
La California 40
La Catarata de Fortuna 80
La Garita 45
La Guácima 47, 49
La Lecheria, Monteverde 88
La Negrita 93
La Selva Biological Research Station 77
La Uvita 63
Lake Arenal 80, 82, **83**
Lake Cachi 54
language 25, 123, 126
Lankester Gardens 54
Las Baulas Marine National Park 102
Las Ruinas, Cartago 53
Liberia 94
Limón Province 61
lithic spheres **16**, 39, 116
llanuras 75
Los Yoses 40

mammals 11, 47, 77, 86, 93, 97, 106, 114, 118
manatee 66, 72
mangroves 102, 105, 110, 111, 115
Manuel Antonio National Park **8**, **108**, 109, **114**
Manzanillo 66
Marine Zoological Museum 50
Marino Ballena National Park 115
Mata de Limón 111
Mawamba Lodge 67
mestizos 24
Moín 63
money 124
monkeys 11, 12, 47, 64, 72, 78, 97, 102, 106, 118
Monte de la Cruz 51
Monteverde **85**, 85-88
Monteverde Butterfly Farm 88
Monteverde Cloud Forest Reserve **74**, 75, 85-87
Monteverde Conservation League 86
Montezuma **104**, **105**
Monumento Nacional Guayabo 16, 57
Moravia 50
Morazan Park 37
Mt Chirripó 5, 9, 28, 109, 115, 116
Museo Criminológico 40
Museo de Arte Costarricense 41
Museo de Arte y Diseño Contemporaneo 38
Museo de Ciencias Naturales 41
Museo de Entomologia 41
Museo de los Niños 40
Museo de Oro Precolombino 36
Museo del Sabanero 95
Museo Ferrocarril 39
Museo Joyas del Trópico Húmedo 51
Museo Nacional 39
Museum of Religious Art 55
Museum of the World's Volcanoes 80

National Cultural Centre 37
national parks 10, 15, 21
Nicoya Peninsula 8, 91, 98, 100, 110
Nosara 92, 100, 103

October Carnival, Puerto Limón **63**
orchids 10, 54, **55**

Orosí Valley **54**
Orotina 110, 111
Osa Peninsula 8
Ostional National Wildlife Refuge 103
Otoya 40
ox carts **26**, 48

Palmar Norte 116
Palo Verde National Park 93, 99
Papagayo Project 91, 100-101
Paquera 104
Parismina 67
Parque España 37
Parque Internacional La Amistad 120
Parrita **111**, 112
Perry, Donald 78
Playa Bonita 63
Playa Conchal **101**
Playa del Coco 101
Playa Espadilla 113
Playa Flamingo 101
Playa Grande **100**, 101, 106
Playa Nancite 96
Playa Naranjo 104
Playa Negra 64
Playa Ocotal 101
Playa Ostional 100, 103
Playa Pavones 120
Playa Sámara 103
Plaza de la Cultura 34, **36**
Protestantism 61
Puerto Hamburgo 62
Puerto Humo 99
Puerto Limón 62, 63, 64
Puerto Limón Carnival 63
Puerto Vargas 64
Puerto Viejo de Sarapiquí 71, 75, 76
Puerto Viejo de Talamanca 66, **67**
Punta Uva 66
Puntarenas 109

Quakers 85
Quepos 15, **113**
quetzal 13, **14**, 53, 87, 97

racoons 47
rain forests **4**, 10, **11**, **77**
Rancho El Trapiche 88
raptors 14
Rara Avis 75, 77
Reserva Natural Absoluta Cabo Blanco 106
restaurants 42, 59, 73, 89, 107, 121
Rincón de la Vieja National Park 96, 97

Río Colorado 71
Río Corobicí 94
Río Frío 84
Río Lagarto 85
Río Pacuaré 57
Río Reventazón 7, 54, 67
Río San Juan 71, 75, 76
Río Sarapiquí 76
Río Sierpe **117**
Río Tempisque 98
Río Turrialba 57
Roman Catholicism 5, 25

Sabana Park 41
Salsa Brava wave 66
Sámara 93, 100
San Carlos (*see* Ciudad Quesada)
San Gerardo de Rivas 115
San Joaquín de Heredia 51
San José 18, **21**, **32**, 33-43
San José de la Montaña 51
San Miguel 79
San Pedro 33, 40
San Ramón 47
Santa Barbara 51
Santa Cruz 98
Santa Elena 85
Santa Elena Cloud Forest Reserve 85
Santa Rosa National Park 96
Santamaria, Juan 46
Sarchí **44**, 48
scuba diving 27, 101, 109
Selva Verde 75, 78
Serpentario 37
Serpentarium, Monteverde 88
Servicio de Parques Nacionales (SPN) 21
sharks 70, 118
Si a Paz 84
Siquirres 62
sloths 11, 46, 63, 64, 70, 72, **76**, 77, 106
Snake Farm 51
snakes 12, 78, **87**, 88, 118
snorkelling 27, 65, 66, 104
sodas 30
Spirogyra Jardin de Mariposas 40, 49
SPN (*see* Servicio de Parques Nacionales)
sportfishing 15, 28, 61, 66, 67, 72, 91, 100, 101, 113, 117, 118, 120
surfing **27**, 64, 66, 91, 96, 100, 101, 102, 105, 109, 113, 117
swimming 28, 63, 69, 70, 102, 103, 105, 106, 110, 112

Tabacón Hot Springs Resort 80
Tamarindo **90**, **103**
Tamarindo Estuary **102**
Tambor 100, 105
Tapantí National Park 55
tapirs 11, 97
Teatro Nacional 33, **35**
Tempisque Ferry 93
Térraba 7
ticos 5, 24, 63
Tilarán 83
Tortuguero **6**, **68**
Tortuguero National Park 61, 62, 67, **69**, **70**
toucans 66
Tourist Information Office (ICT) 34, 122
transport 125
travelling to Costa Rica 123
Turrialba 57, 62
turtles 12, 66, 69, 70, 96, 101, 103, 104, 118

Ujarras 54
Universidad Nacional 50
University of Costa Rica 40

Valle de Diquis 116
Valle de El General 109, 116
Vara Blanca 49
Vásquez de Coronado, Juan 18
Venado Caves 83
Volcán Arenal 6, 75, **80**, 87
Volcán Barva 7, 50, 52, 76
Volcán Irazú 6, 45, **56**, **57**
Volcán Orosí 6, **7**, 91
Volcán Poás 6, 45, 48, 76
Volcán Rincón de la Vieja 6, 91
Volcán Santa María 6, 91
Volcán Turrialba 57
volcanoes 6, 7, 91

Walker, William **18**, 19, 96
walking trails 64, 66, 77, 78, 86, 91, 96
Waterfall Lodge 78
whales 15, 115
white-water rafting 28, 57, 78, 94, 113
wildcats 11, 13
wildlife 69, 77, 91, 99, 106, 114, 120
Wilson Botanical Gardens 119
windsurfing 27, 80, 83

Zarcero 26
Zoo-Ave 47